The Recruiters
LinkedIn Lead Rush

The Quick and Dirty Secrets for any Serious Recruitment and Search Business Owner who wants to attract a Rush of Clients and Candidates with LinkedIn

Terry Edwards

The Recruiters LinkedIn Leadrush

Copyright © 2016 Terry Edwards

www.drewcoaching.com

First published in Great Britain in 2016 by Compass Publishing

ISBN 978-1-907308-43-7

Set by The Book Refinery Ltd

Printed and bound in the UK by CMP.

Testimonials

 *"Happy to say that I have won business from putting Terry's methods into practice so I have no hesitation in recommending him to non-competitors especially if they are in a different geographical location!"*

Richard Blann
RandKA Flexible Recruitment Solutions

 *"Terry has an engaging style and a unique outside-the-box approach to recruiting methodologies, which I appreciate. Continually being open to new ideas, communication styles and techniques related to our business is important given the ever-changing climate of the business environment."*

Joe S. Murawski
Focused Hire

 *"I have owned my own recruitment firm for 14 years now, and I must say I was reluctant to engage drewcoaching as I questioned if I would get my monies worth, also I believed that if there is anything that needs doing to improve the performance of the business then I would do it. However, what I have found with working with drewcoaching is, I am more focused than at any other time in my career. It is also great to have a sounding board to vent some of my frustration that come with running a recruitment business. The main advantage of engaging drewcoaching is my marketing knowledge has increased substantially and our sales have improved dramatically. If you are looking to increase sales and the performance of your team, I would recommend drewcoaching..."*

Eloise Shelton
Vanilla Recruitment

"I have been a recruitment business owner for 15 years and in that time I have met numerous coaches and trainers. I wasn't keen at first to work with drewcoaching as I  thought that after nearly 15 years in the business, there was little else I could learn about building a recruitment business. Another concern was the fact that I would be sharing my company's details with someone who works with many of my competitors. Since working with drewcoaching, I have experienced an amazing transformation in business development. As a business we are able to generate more sales enquiries than ever in the history of the business and all of them without ever making a cold call. In fact, we generated 82 leads in 4 days and signed one retained assignment, which when you consider we don't really sell retained recruitment, that was quite an achievement. The marketing has been so successful that potential clients are calling us, we have had to put the marketing on stop as we are unable to cope with so many leads in a short period of time. If you are tired of cold calling and would like to discover how to have your clients calling you, I would recommend drewcoaching."

Steve Hauge
Foundation Resourcing

 *"I appointed Terry in October 2010 as my Business Coach and since that day I have never looked back. He has been motivating in both my business life and at home. He has helped me find the focus I needed to see through all of the everyday 'firefighting' that can 'cloud' your judgement and made me realise that by taking responsibility for your actions and in-actions everyday, you will achieve your goals. 'Goals' is also another watch word with Terry, without them there is no destination and whilst anyone can set goals, Terry will enable you to exceed them in every way. In addition to the weekly coaching sessions, he is always available to provide guidance at the end of the phone. His knowledge of marketing, has made a significant difference to the results I am seeing in my business. Terry you are an inspiration and a star."*

Melanie Bose
Omnium IT Recruitment Limited

"I find the marketing tips and information Terry shares interesting and I really get a lot of value and benefit from them. I have often forwarded them on to others and  just find them a good read, not too much information and not too long and "waffling." I find that I feel like I know who you are, I really enjoy your writing. I would be happy to recommend Terry to other Recruitment/Search Firms... I work closely with a number of other Recruiters and Search firms and I find that in this economy we need to, and benefit from, working together. I do a number of splits with other agencies and I think we need to change how we see and do things. I have been so grateful to be able to get help and to give help to other colleagues, I think we all need to get an "abundance" mentality... let's all work together and share... Half a loaf of bread is far better than no bread at all."

Debra Manson
Debra Manson Recruitment & Training

"22 leads in just 5 days... Without making a single cold call! – Terry delivers what he says he's going to and that's all you can ask for..."

Kate Bailey
Cranleigh Personnel

"Terry provides a friendly voice giving me insights into the recruitment industry and ideas on marketing based on his no-nonsense, problem solving approach."

Richard Brown
Grassroots Recruitment

Introduction

If you've got a LinkedIn account, but you're struggling to generate leads and you're frustrated at the number you know you're missing out on but you don't yet know how to attract them and you know just one small but important step in the right direction - one last small piece of the *'LinkedIn marketing puzzle'* - is going to be enough to make it all start happening for you, then this book is going to make your life a lot better, and your business a lot more **profitable.**

Because regardless of the competition, recession or the economy, the truth is your LinkedIn Account can be your own personal **'gold mine'**.

BUT this is only true if you master a small number of simple skills and put some very easily copied LinkedIn strategies to work for you in your *Recruitment/Search Business.*

And this book is going to tell you exactly how to do it. But before I do that, I want to make sure this book is really for you. In fact, I want to put you off reading any further. Why? Well, I'm going to demand two things from you; firstly, a **modest investment** towards the future success of your business, and secondly, a **commitment** from you to put in the time to make these changes.

And if you're not the kind of person that is willing to invest in either of these elements, then this book isn't for you and reading it will just be a waste of your time.

A comment often quoted when it comes to LinkedIn is;

"My clients/candidates are not on LinkedIn so I don't use it."

I would agree and say that not everyone is on LinkedIn and anyone that tells you differently is not telling the truth.

LinkedIn is just a social media platform that you should at least test to see how many leads you generate using it, and test and see how many candidate you could find on LinkedIn.

The average Recruitment/Search Firm uses these methods for getting NEW business:

1. Cold calling.

2. Word of mouth.

3. MPC - Most Placeable Candidate.

4. Referrals.

5. Hope Marketing (this is where you hope that clients and candidates will contact you).

In total there are over 147 different methods that you as a Recruitment/Search firm owner can use to get business.

Tell me... if you are using FIVE methods to generate leads and your competitors are using FIFTY methods to generate leads, who do you think will get the most leads?

Silly question really...

Also, a quick heads up;

My opinion doesn't matter.

Your opinion doesn't matter.

Your partner's opinion doesn't matter.

There are a lot of people out there who will give you their opinion, whether you want it or not.

They will say things like...

"Social media marketing is just a fad."

"I wouldn't work with someone I met via LinkedIn."

You may even say or think...

"My clients are too sophisticated."

Or the worst one...

"Yeah, but my market is different."

Quite frankly nobody's opinion counts, all that counts are the results.

So regardless of what you or your trusted adviser thinks is going to work, TEST IT! Yep and **TEST it again**.

The fact is, what you are about to discover has already been used by some of the most successful Search and Recruitment firms in the world.

If you do what successful Recruitment and Search Firm Owners do, you will get what successful Recruitment and Search Firm owners get
*~ **Terry Edwards***

What's more, this book is definitely NOT for you if:

1. **You believe that this — or anything else for that matter — is going to work for you without putting in ANY effort.**

If you think that, then you're reading the wrong message and listening to the wrong person. Make no mistake about it. To grow a successful Recruitment/Search Business there will be a substantial amount of work involved. But trust me, it will be worth it!

I'm telling you now, right up front, if you take this next step, then you're letting yourself in for some serious hard work. Don't continue if that puts you off — because that's exactly what I'm going to get you to do.

2. **You're not serious about increasing the number of leads you generate and the number of candidates you attract with LinkedIn.**

The fact is, most Recruitment/Search Businesses DON'T generate the amount of leads that they should, but with just a few tweaks to your LinkedIn marketing campaign you will see a dramatic increase in the number of prospects you're able to attract.

If you're the kind of person I'm looking for, you will discover how your Recruitment/Search Business, will become a leading player in your sector and, in some cases, a leading player worldwide.

Obviously I cannot guarantee these results, but as you read this book, I AM promising you a substantial increase in your leads and sales, and it's a promise I'm backing up with my own time and money.

3. **You're unwilling to change what you're currently doing.**

The truth is, IF what you're doing now isn't getting the results you want, it never will. To get better results, you need to start doing things differently. If you're not willing to do that, then please don't bother wasting both our time because this really isn't for you.

So, if you're still with me, then you're serious about wanting a dramatic improvement in your Recruitment/Search Business and you're prepared to knuckle down and work up a good sweat so that it happens.

And you're exactly the kind of person I want to join me.

So, who am I and why should you care?

I'm Terry Edwards, lead generation and Recruitment marketing expert. A.K.A. *'The Renegade Recruiter.'*

When I first entered the Recruitment world over 27 years ago, I joined one of the leading IT Search Firms at that time. I had no Recruitment experience, but I had worked in HR Training and Development.

I was given a Rolodex and told to get on the phone and start prospecting for business. That was exactly what I did and it worked. I would cold call IT Directors and HR Directors and tell them what a great firm we were and what a great job we could do for them finding top performing IT professionals.

Don't get me wrong, that method worked and we would bill 200k - 300k per year, every year. As I said though, that was over 27 years ago and things have significantly changed since then.

For example, in my day I would fax a CV to my client and I would also have to post it as the fax copy would fade. In fact, in our company we had a post room to handle the hundreds of CVs that would go out on a daily basis.

The good old days....

I then set up my own Recruitment Business.

The first 12 months was an absolute disaster!

In fact, we only billed 52k in that period, when previously we would regularly bill 60k in a quarter. To say I was disillusioned and frustrated is an understatement.

I was then fortunate enough to meet a Business Mentor who shared some words with me that would go on to change my life.

He said...

"Your success as a Recruitment Business owner has nothing to do with how good you are as a Recruiter, it has everything to do with how good you are at attracting clients and candidates."

He explained that to be successful as a Recruitment Business owner, you have to master Marketing. It was at *this point* that I was forced to take a step back and take a deeper look at what was going on. I then realised a few important things that changed our lives forever.

The first big realisation for us was in regarded to the marketing approach we were using.

Basically we had *four main ways of getting business.*

The first one was to '**cold call**'. In most cases calling complete and utter strangers and asking them to spend £10-15K with me. As I mentioned earlier, it worked, but it could be 'bloody' hard work and I didn't enjoy making those calls. In all the time I did it, I never had a hiring manager thank me for *interrupting* them with my calls.

The other method was '**word of mouth**'. This is where someone would call me having heard about us from one of our existing clients. Now this was very nice, but sadly it didn't happen very often. It was also very reactive and I had very little control over who and when they called.

We also used **referrals** for getting business, again this was very haphazard and we didn't have any real system in place for getting referrals.

A real winner for us was marketing out a 'Good candidate' I say it was a real winner, in as much as if the prospect had a need for that type of candidate they would respond. The downside was, the client would never want to work on a retainer for future business. The consequence of which were relationships with clients who quite frankly didn't really appreciate the service we offered.

The worst and sadly the most common method we used was '**hope marketing**'. This is where we kind of 'hoped' that clients would come banging on our door with their credit card in their hands. As you can imagine that didn't happen very often either, it really is a crazy way to try and get business. However, *a lot* of Recruitment/Search Business owners RELY on that method.

So those were our four methods for getting business. Did you know there are actually 147 different ways that you can do this?

When we found this out, we embarked on what is fondly called '**brand advertising**'.

Every marketing message we sent out was designed to *raise awareness* for the company.

It was heavily focused on the logo, company colours and our mission statement. In fact, it's very similar to what you see today from the majority of Recruitment/Search Business owners.

All in the hope that it's somehow going to attract the right attention and result in more business.

The problem with that is, most of the time people aren't actually *looking for you or your services*. They're looking for a 'headache cure' rather than 'aspirin'. So if you go around marketing 'aspirin', with all its fancy colours and logos, more often than not it gets ignored!

All your prospects really care about is themselves and their problems.

That's why one of the biggest mistakes you can make as a Recruitment/Search Business owner, is having your marketing messages plastered with YOUR logo and YOUR company details and YOUR 'amazing' qualities. It's a waste of time, paper and ink.

This becomes even more important when talking about LinkedIn or social media in general, because there's always the danger of spending hours of your day engaging in 'brand advertising' without it ever resulting in money in your bank account. This is something I'll address in more detail later on in this book.

It's not about engagement...it's about leads!

Discovering this obvious but very important lesson caused us to make a complete shift in the way we approached things.

Going forward, everything we did on LinkedIn was for the sole purpose of *lead generation*. And if any activity could not be directly attributed to the acquisition of more leads then we stopped doing it completely. Put very simply, it meant that if we did something and it worked, we would have more leads in our pipeline, and if we didn't have leads in our pipeline, then what we were doing wasn't working, so we stopped doing it. Very simple, but it made all the difference.

Applying this philosophy to LinkedIn changed everything!

Having read countless books and articles on LinkedIn and attending training seminars and events, it became apparent that none of them were teaching this **'direct response approach' (DR)**. Every training course I took on LinkedIn, and everything I read on the subject, was all about the *mechanics* of LinkedIn. How it worked, how to use the functions it offers, but there was nothing about strategies, of generating LEADS, so that prospects were raising their hands and indicating they had an interest in using a Recruitment/Search firm.

That's where this book is different.

Because of the lack of training and information out there, I felt I had no choice but to take matters into my own hands and figure out what the most successful Recruitment/ Search Business owners from around the world were doing to generate leads, win business and increase their personal earnings.

So I spoke to these top Recruitment/Search Business owners and asked them this question, *"What is the secret to get LinkedIn to make money for you and your business?"*

Some of them were reluctant to reveal their secrets whilst others were more than happy to tell me everything that they did.

We then took the strategies that were being used by the

most successful Recruitment/Search Business owners and shared them with other Recruitment/Search Business owners, and they too achieved very similar results.

Since then, these methods have been used by hundreds of Recruitment/Search Business owners from around the world and it has always resulted in more leads, more business and more money for the owner of the business.

Within just two weeks of applying one of these strategies, a client of mine in the USA, generated 97 leads in **FOUR** days and signed two clients worth an additional $60,000 in business revenue!

Another client of ours in the UK, within three weeks of using the system, acquired **five** new clients worth over £100,000 in business profits.

These results aren't necessarily typical. Obviously, a lot depends on your market, your work ethic and your wherewithal.

I can't guarantee what outcome you'll get if you implement these strategies without having a better understanding of you and your business, but I can promise you this: read this book, **put the strategies I teach into practice** and if you're not happy with the results, simply email my office at info@driesching.com and I'll refund every penny you paid for it. And I'll even let you keep the book too! I can't say much fairer than that, can I?

What's the difference that makes the difference?

For the best part of half a decade, I've dedicated my time to finding out what the top performing Recruitment/Search

Business owners in the world do differently from everybody else.

Why is it that some Recruitment/Search businesses are extremely successful and then at the same time, in the same market, selling what is pretty much the same service, there is another Recruitment/Search Business struggling to get by and can't seem to generate the income they want or attract the clients they need?

What I've found is, the really successful Recruitment/Search business owners aren't any more intelligent than anybody else, they don't have a better service; they're not even necessarily better at what they do, but the one thing they **do have**, *is a working, reliable and predictable system* for bringing in clients and candidates, generating leads and increasing business profits.

I now spend my time sharing this *exact system* with recruitment business owners all over the world, so *you* can get similar results and transform your business too. Not correct.

My clients include some of the world's most successful Recruitment/Search Businesses on both sides of the Atlantic, and every month, Recruitment/Search Business owners from all over the world attend our online seminars, events and video training programmes. Over 10 thousand Recruitment/Search Business owners receive my business growth tips via email on a daily basis.

If I were you, I would ask yourself this question, "*Is there a reason why so many of the world's top performing Recruitment/Search Business owners, so regularly take Terry's advice and put it into practice in their businesses?"*

Of course there is. And I can assure you it's NOT because

of my age, charm or good looks. No, it's because I get results. And in the marketing game, that's what counts and it's <u>ALL that counts.</u>

Now, the reason I'm sharing this with you is not to brag.

It's so you can see that when I say I'm sharing something **powerful and profitable with you**, then it's worth your while taking notice.

Mindset matters

I recently saw a poster of Indian businessman, investor and philanthropist Rata Tata with the words:

"No one can destroy iron, but its own rust can! Likewise, no one can destroy a person, but his own mindset can."

I believe everyone has the chance to succeed and it's only what's in your head that STOPS you from achieving your goals.

Whenever we talk about effective Recruitment/Search Business marketing we have to also talk about goals.

The first step in the marketing process for a Recruitment/Search Business is to clarify what you want to accomplish. Many Recruitment/Search Businesses ultimately fail because their marketing objectives are too vague

In other words, if your only objective is a certain level of sales volume and income then you're building your business on shifting sand rather than a solid foundation.

Hitting high sales volumes (as a goal) is actually pretty easy if that's all you want to do. It starts to get difficult when you begin interlocking that objective with other objectives, such as a certain amount of profit margins and retained earnings, a certain level of quality in services and niche markets.

One owner I got to know really well built a three million pound company from scratch in five years. He made a statement that has stuck with me ever since.

"Making a million pounds was the easiest thing I ever did. Believing it could happen to me was the part that took forty one years."

The point I want to make is, making a lot of money is more dependent on *your beliefs* and what your *goals* are, than any other factor.

You see, if you don't know where you are going, then any road will take you there.

So, answer these simple yet profound questions before we go any further.

1. **What would your business look like if you knew you could not fail?**

2. **When will that be?**

Why LinkedIn?

Because you've picked up this book, I'm going to make the assumption you're at least curious about what LinkedIn can do for you and your business.

If you are anything like the majority of Recruitment/Search Business owners we speak to on a regular basis, you're probably already using it now and want to get better results. Maybe you're completely new to it, have no idea how or why it works, but you know it's something that has massive potential for your business if you can just discover how to use it in the right way.

Well fantastic!

Because that's exactly my intention. But first, just in case you still need convincing as to why you should be testing LinkedIn as a source of new prospects in your business, here are a few numbers you should be aware of:

> According to www.expandedramblings.com, in an article first published in February 2015, LinkedIn has over 346 million users. It has a user growth of two new members per second, and the LinkedIn website has 187 million unique visitors every single month.

> It has a geographical reach of over 200 countries and territories, and 40% of all users check LinkedIn daily.

Now let's take a look at those numbers in a bit more detail to see how they could directly effect your business.

If LinkedIn has over 346 million users, and just 0.001% of those became your clients, that would be equal to 3,460 new customers.

Now, I'm aware that not every LinkedIn user will be in your target market, but even conservatively, there would be a high enough margin of those 346 million users that would fit your target audience to make it a very profitable tool.

And remember, it's growing by two new members every single second. That equates to 1,200 new members joining, in the same time you've taken to read this section of the book.

Sticking with the 0.001% example, this could mean a new prospect in your market joins every single day. (I realise that without the actual number of people in your target audience using LinkedIn, the math behind those numbers is guesswork, but it's certainly worth thinking about.)

LinkedIn has a geographic reach of over 200 countries and territories. That means that whatever country your target audience operates in, it's very likely that LinkedIn has it covered.

And 40% of LinkedIn users check the site daily. Again, using the 0.001% example, that would mean that 1,384 of *your* clients or prospects would be visiting the site every single day. And you have the power to get your message in front of them.

That's powerful stuff and could prove to be a big breakthrough in your business.

Part 1:
What's the Real
Purpose of Using LinkedIn?

"I realised that becoming a master of karate was not about learning 4,000 moves, but about doing just a handful of moves 4,000 times."
Chet Holmes ~ The Ultimate Sales Machine

The truth about Social Media

A lot has been said about social media over the past few years. It seems to have emerged almost out of nowhere as the 'in' thing for business owners to be doing. All of a sudden, there were so called 'gurus' and 'experts' popping up all over the place selling social media marketing as the number one thing you must be doing if you wanted your business to survive. Even though decades before social media existed, businesses were operating just fine. And even years after its initial boom, you'll still find thousands of very profitable businesses being successful without it.

In contrast to these 'gurus', you have the sceptics and non-believers who doubt the whole social media concept. These are the types of people who believe it's a fad, as if platforms like Facebook, LinkedIn and Twitter could disappear overnight without any warning

I'm neither of these. I don't and never will class myself as a 'social media guru' and I don't believe that the information and strategies in this book are crucial for your business to survive.

There is more than one way to skin a cat. However, if more leads and more clients are what you're looking for, then using these strategies – like we have in our business, as well as many others – could certainly help you achieve that.

No one can say for certain how long LinkedIn will be around for, but what I do know for certain is that it is here now. So we intend to profit from it while we can, and you should too.

What I can say without any doubt is that if you use social media like the majority of Recruitment/Search Business owners out there, you're wasting your time. Quite simply, there are methods that work and methods that don't. But most of what you read, see and hear on the subject fall into the latter category, and it's my wish to see you achieve measured success from a tested approach.

Activity Vs. Results

There's a danger with all forms of marketing, but especially with social media marketing, of getting too bogged down in 'activity'. I see it all the time, Recruitment/Search Business owners who hear about the riches that LinkedIn holds and so dedicate every spare hour of their day to just doing stuff on LinkedIn. And if that 'stuff' is not being measured and tested, then you're better off doing nothing at all.

This following example isn't LinkedIn specific, but the message can be easily translated...

I'll often meet business owners from all industries who boast about how many Facebook likes they have or how many followers they have on Twitter. They become obsessed with it, spending every spare minute of their day working on the goal of getting more likes, or new followers. And although there are a few industries where Facebook likes and Twitter followers may be useful, for most people it's a complete waste of time. How much is a Facebook 'like' worth in business revenue? How's a Twitter follower going to add profits to your bottom line?

Some businesses will be able to answer that question with confidence, but they are very few. For most, a Facebook 'like' or a Twitter follower does nothing to boost profits and only serves as an ego boost.

If you're engaging in an activity to boost your ego - then fair enough - but ego boosts don't pay your overheads, your staff, or fund nice holidays.

I fell into a similar trap when I first started using LinkedIn. I had read somewhere that the power of LinkedIn was in your network. *"The more connections you have, the more chance you've got of making a sale."* - true to a certain point, but having a huge list of LinkedIn contacts is no different to having a huge following on Twitter. The key is to find a way to **monetise those assets**.

In this book, we're going to be looking at two categories (or types) of marketing on LinkedIn. One is what I call *'organic marketing'*, and the other is *'paid advertising'*.

We'll look at these two categories in more detail, but for now there's one important fact about both of them that you need to understand. Although given their names it may seem like one of these methods is free and the other is paid for, that's not quite the case. Yes, one of these methods is paid for in monetary value, but the other is paid for in time. There is always a price to pay!

That being said, it's vital that everything we do on LinkedIn - whether we pay for it in time or money - is profitable. It's vital that we get a *return on investment!* So we can't afford to engage in any activity that doesn't get us results.

There's a saying I heard very early on in my career, *"If it can't be measured, it can't be managed."* And there's a lot of truth in that. Every activity you engage in on LinkedIn should be measurable by way of the results you're getting.

To put it very simply, if you cannot clearly say 'activity Y leads to result X' and know for sure that result X is a profitable one, then you should not be engaging in activity Y.

LinkedIn, as with all forms of marketing, should be 100% results focused.

Taking a 'direct response' approach to LinkedIn

There are two *styles* of marketing. (Be careful that you don't confuse **types** of marketing, which I mentioned earlier, and **styles** of marketing, which is what I'm explaining now.) And if you're finding that your marketing isn't getting a response, it might be because you're engaging in one rather than the other.

The **two styles** of marketing are:

1. Brand advertising.

2. Direct response marketing.

You see, most Recruitment/Search Business owners engage in what's commonly known as **'brand advertising'**.

Remember in the introduction, I mentioned that we were focusing our efforts on our logo being seen, and company colours? Well, brand advertising is all about getting you; your brand; the company colours and logo out there for the world to see, in the hope that it's somehow going to attract the right attention and cause people to give you their business.

The problem with that is that most of the time, your prospects aren't actually looking for you or your services at all.

Remember my analogy of 'aspirin' vs. 'headache cure'? So if you go around marketing your brand of 'aspirin' with all its fancy colours and logos, more often than not it gets ignored, because why would people choose your brand over everyone else's?

Remember, all your prospects really care about is themselves and their problems...

That's why, as I mentioned earlier, one of the biggest mistakes you can make as a Recruitment/Search Business owners is to have your marketing messages focused on YOUR logo and YOUR company details and how long you've been in business.

Why?

Because no one cares!

The only thing your potential clients are interested in is how *effective your product is in curing their problem.*

The only marketing you should be doing is 'direct response

marketing'. That is, every single marketing activity you engage in should be for one reason and one reason only...to get a **direct response** from the potential client.

This may include:

> ➤ Picking up the phone to call you.

> ➤ Coming into your office.

> ➤ Filling out a form on your website (usually to get more information).

Whatever it is you want them to do!

You get direct, clear and measurable responses.

And that's the other thing about brand advertising, it's all but impossible to measure. A million people could see your company name and logo, but you'd have no way of knowing whether or not any of them would buy from you off the back of it!

Think about your typical television ad, for instance. I'm not talking about infomercials, where there is often a very clear and precise call to action making it 'Direct response marketing';

I'm talking about the typical television ad that you might see from the likes of Coca-Cola around Christmas time. This is a prime example of 'Brand advertising'. This often costs millions to do and is something that most small businesses in any industry can't afford - sure, you'll get to see their logo and their company name, but does this equal more sales? I suspect not, and even if sales did happen to go up during the period the ad was being displayed, there's no way of knowing whether people were buying directly off the back of it.

And that's not to say that branding doesn't have a place, because it does, but it should be a by-product of your *'direct response'* marketing.

Brand advertising does not equal leads...but direct response marketing does!

We'll be applying the 'direct response' thinking to everything we do on LinkedIn, so it's important we get this fundamental lesson out of the way nice and early. Even if the above is something you already know at some level, there is no harm in a gentle reminder.

Getting people off LinkedIn and onto a media *you* control

Before I go any further, I need to make an observation, and that is: this is a book and LinkedIn is a website. With a click of a few buttons, LinkedIn could make changes to its platform that could render all of this information out of date. Writing and publishing a book takes time, and LinkedIn could decide to make its next set of changes instantly.

That being said, there is one overall purpose we must do on LinkedIn that will remain constant. So if you only take one thing away from this book make sure it's this: The purpose of marketing on LinkedIn is to get your potential clients **off** LinkedIn and onto a platform that you control.

What I mean is that LinkedIn can make changes at any time. Literally overnight. For example, at the time of writing this, you are able to message your contacts through LinkedIn. There's no guarantee that you will be able to do that tomorrow. You are also able to participate in group discussions, but there's no guarantee that you will be able to do that in the future. Currently, LinkedIn stores all of your 'connections' on its platform so you can access them whenever you want, there's no guarantee that you will be able to do that tomorrow.

LinkedIn will always be changing its functionality, but the purpose of LinkedIn for you as a Recruitment/Search Business owner (who uses it for marketing purposes) will always stay the same: Get people off it, and onto a marketing platform you control. (And when I say off it, I don't mean for them to stop using it, I simply mean get their details and permission to communicate with them directly via an alternative media.)

LinkedIn is a goldmine, but it's not the only one.

When I first discovered LinkedIn, I became addicted to it. Using it to market my business became the primary activity of my day, every day, even at the weekends. And it worked. I'll share the specifics with you throughout this book, but understand that it got me results and continues to get me results even today.

LinkedIn can and will be a profit goldmine for your business too, but remember it's not the only platform out there...

I previously talked about how LinkedIn can change things at any given moment and up until now, the only consequences of this has been that I've had to tweak and modify the methods I use, but the basic process has stayed the same.

To date, LinkedIn hasn't made a change that has made my strategies obsolete. But that doesn't mean they won't. A lot of the time, the changes they make actually benefit you as a business owner but that doesn't mean it will stay that way.

This means you need to mine the profits available to you while you can, understanding that this 'goldmine' could end tomorrow.

Always remember that at any given moment, LinkedIn could shut you down and cut your profits off at source. It's happened in many other industries before now and social media is no different. I remember a few years back when SEO was all the rage. There were thousands of businesses that built their foundations on the basis that Google would send free traffic to their website. They relied totally on Google sending them all of their business. Then all of a sudden, overnight, Google decided to change their algorithms (the code behind the search results) and boom - literally overnight these businesses stopped getting traffic to their websites. And because these businesses relied on Google so much, it had devastating results. Gone, wiped out, because Google decided to change the coding behind their platform.

I once worked with a client who used telemarketing as their only route to market. It worked well for years and then gradually it became harder and harder to get through to people. The less people she got through to, the less profit she made. No profits meant no business... gone! Wiped out because people got sick of receiving cold calls and gatekeepers became better at keeping them out.

I can give you an endless list of examples where businesses have relied on one source for getting clients only for the source to dry up and put them out of business. Don't make the same mistake!

Nearly every business owner I speak to has one thing in common, and that is they long for *one simple thing* they can do so they can develop a secure business with enough profit to sustain itself and give them the life they want.

There's no doubt that this can be achieved, but not by doing or relying on one source of garnering prospects.

I remember once hearing the story of a fisherman in Hawaii from Dan Kennedy's book '*No B.S. Price Strategy*'.

A man was relaxing on the beach in Hawaii, soaking up the sun and watching the waves crash against the shore in the distance, when a local fisherman drove up in his pick-up truck. He got out with a dozen fishing rods, not one, but a dozen.

He then baited each hook, cast all the lines into the ocean and set the rods in the sand.

Intrigued, the man wandered over and asked him for an explanation.

His reply:

"*It's simple. I love fish, but I hate fishing. I like eating, not catching, so I cast 12 lines. By sunset, some of them will have caught a fish, never all of 'em. So if I only cast one or two lines, I might go hungry, but 12 is enough to always catch some. Usually there's enough for me, and extras to sell to local restaurants. This way I live the life I want.*"

Sounds like a very simplistic approach, but your business should be run in pretty much the same way.

In this metaphor, each fishing rod represents a method for bringing in new business.

Some will catch...

Others will not.

But overall, you'll attract enough clients and candidates to enable you to live the life you want.

The problem for most Recruitment/Search Business owners is that they rely on just one fishing rod, one method for attracting clients and candidates.

Some Recruitment/Search Business owners will have picked up this book in the hope of finding that 'one thing' that's going to make all the difference. There's a very good chance LinkedIn will help you make a 'catch'. But you still need to make sure you have other fishing rods baited and hooked, otherwise you could go hungry.

Remember, LinkedIn could change things overnight, which means it's no longer viable to use it as a marketing tool. There's talk of it moving into the Recruitment/Staffing space, and to offer this service as the primary function of its platform. This means that rather than being a networking site as it is now, it would be a job site and recruit for companies using the information it has on the profiles of its members. What does that mean for us?

So bear that in mind before you start relying on it as the only 'fishing rod' you have in the sea.

Part 2:
Your LinkedIn
Audience

*"Your LinkedIn profile must be 100% client focused.
In order to ensure that this is the case, the first step
requires that you get a clear picture of
who your ideal client is."*
Melonie Dodaro ~ The LinkedIn Code

The importance of knowing who you're targeting

One thing that strikes me about the Recruitment/Search Business owners who are struggling to attract all the clients they want is that they don't actually know who their ideal client is.

Sure, they may have some inkling as to what market they operate in, but I'm talking about a careful analysis of their target client.

Top Recruitment/Search Business owners have a very strict set of criteria that a potential client must meet before they'll even get into a conversation with them, and this really pays because it means they don't have to spend any time with the tire kickers.

Recruitment/Search Business owners are happy to work with anyone, as long as they have the ability to pay, and some people won't even set an ability to pay as a requirement. (It always leaves a sick feeling in the bottom of my stomach when I hear of Recruitment/Search Business owners doing something they're good at, for free.)

FACT

The average Contingency Recruitment/Search Business will complete 25% of the job orders that they work on. That means 75% of the time they are working, they will never ever get paid for what they are doing. On the other hand, the average Retained Recruitment/Search Business, will fill 95% of their job orders. As a consequence, Retained Recruitment/Search Business owners work less, but earn much more.

Most Contingency Recruitment/Search Business owners think that they can't control who they attract to their business, and because they're so desperate for any and every client they can get, they will have *anyone*.

If you think that, then you're dead wrong.

The top performers don't just go after anybody. They're very selective about who they do business with, because they know that doing business with the wrong people can end up costing more money than they bring into the business.

There are two types of buyers in your Recruitment/Search Business, these are;

The transactional buyer

1. Transactional buyers are focused *only* on today's transaction and give little thought to the possibility of future purchases.

2. Their only fear is of paying more than they have to pay. Transactional buyers are looking for price and value.

3. They enjoy the process of comparing and negotiating and will likely shop around before making their decision to purchase.

4. Transactional buyers do their own research so they won't need the help of an expert.

5. Because they enjoy the process, transactional buyers don't consider their time spent buying to be part of the purchase price.

6. Anxious to share the 'good deal' they've found, transactional buyers are excellent sources of word-of-mouth advertising.

The relational buyer (your ideal buyer)

1. Relational Buyers considers today's transaction to be one in a long series of many future purchases.

2. Their only fear is of making a poor choice. Relational shoppers will purchase as soon as they have confidence. As the seller, it is your job to give them the confidence they seek

3. They don't particularly enjoy the process of buying and negotiating.

4. Relational shoppers are looking principally for an expert they can trust.

5. They consider their time to be part of the purchase price.

6. Confident that they have found *the right place to buy*, relational buyers are very likely to become repeat customers.

In his book, *'Secret Formulas of the Wizard of Ads'* Roy Williams says that because some buyers will be in transactional mode and others in relational mode, your success or failure hinges on knowing which is which and adjusting your selling style accordingly.

Challenges occur when buyers attempt to engage your Recruitment/Search services using the transactional approach.

This is when the buyer doesn't answer your questions and demands to know your rates, or requests your terms before they fully understand your offering.

If you build a business that is willing to go after just anybody and everybody, it's almost impossible to do unless it's based on price. And this is a losing battle because there will always be someone willing to do it cheaper than you.

Think about it, if you know exactly who your best set of clients are, you can then use those specific demographics to select the people who match up well with that profile, and then invest *all of your marketing efforts to attract only those types of clients.*

And when I say best clients, what I mean is, the people who buy based on the best value rather than the best price. When you have a client list full of only the best, you can't help but have a more profitable business. You work less but earn more, and the people you're working with become long-term friends as well as great business contacts.

This principle applies to marketing through LinkedIn or any other form of media. **You must have a very clear idea of who it is you're targeting.** (Which will in turn, attract your ideal client.)

Sometime ago, I received an email from a guy called Ben Settle. He's a copywriter based in the Sates and I had the pleasure of interviewing him. He had some very useful things to say about marketing, sales and growing a business.

The message from this particular email was that you should be treating your potential clients like criminals.

You see, most of the Recruitment/Search Businesses I speak to want to know how to make more sales. They always ask questions like...

"What are the best sales tricks?" and, *"How do I compel my prospects to buy?"*

But they're asking the wrong questions.

Ben Settle compared it to: *"asking an FBI agent what's more important: being able to shoot a criminal from 200 feet away, or knowing how to profile a criminal so they know where that person is, what their next move will be, how they think and what's the best way to catch them?"*

And that is a very interesting thought, not that your potential clients are criminals (hopefully!), but being able to profile your ideal client so you know everything about them psychologically, demographically, emotionally and even physically, as this could be really helpful in 'catching them'. (Remember our fishing rod metaphor in the last chapter?)

Using this tactic, you should then be able to make more sales and attract more clients, regardless of how good you are at sales, because you'll know where to find them. You'll know exactly what they want, what to say to them and how to deliver your message in the most receptive way.

All the silky sales skills in the world are nothing compared to this!

Going after the right people is vital when it comes to building a profitable LinkedIn marketing system.

Is LinkedIn the right media for your market?

One of the reasons LinkedIn has worked so well for me and the clients I work with, is because before we actually start implementing any strategy, we make sure it fits with the profile of our ideal client.

When engaging in any marketing activity, you need to be sure the media you're going to use reaches your potential clients in a way that resonates with what it is you're trying to sell. The market, message and media match is basic stuff, but so many people get it wrong.

Let me explain. Let's say, for example, you own a business that makes hearing aids for people who are hard of hearing.

Your market, the people you want to work with, are obviously people who are hard of hearing.

Your message is that you're going to *improve* their hearing.

It's a perfect match! Your product *clearly solves* the problem your ideal client is having.

The next step is to get your message out there; you need your market to know what it is that you do. That's where the media comes in. The media is the method you use to communicate with these people. For example, LinkedIn is one form of media, as is email; telephone; print; billboards and websites etc.

All of these will get your message out there. But they will only get the results you want if they match both your message and your market.

I'm going to give you a pretty obvious incongruent match - but I really want to stress the point – so bear with me. If we take our hard of hearing example, and I choose to use radio as my media, then I'm probably not going to get a good response for obvious reasons. I would have a similar problem if I were trying to sell female hair products by putting a poster in a male changing room, or an advert in a men's fitness magazine.

Switch the ad for the hearing aids to a more visual based media, such as a billboard or in print, and I'd get a better response. Switching the poster for the female hair products from the men's changing room to the women's changing room will also see a better response. But remember, just because the poster selling the female hair products didn't get the response I wanted, doesn't necessarily mean that that media doesn't work. You might find that if I sold a different product, such as a solution for male pattern baldness, (and put it in the male changing room) that media might come up trumps.

The message, market and the media must be in sync.

People make mistakes like this all the time and then very quickly jump to the conclusion that it's the message that was wrong, or the product/service wasn't right. But a lot of the time it's just a case of using the wrong media, which means their message doesn't reach their ideal client.

The reason I bring this point up is because LinkedIn will only work for you if it's a media that your target audience uses, and the only way you can know that for sure is to test. You'd be surprised at what you find.

If you've already got a LinkedIn profile or you're familiar with the platform, you'll have noticed that it has a very corporate and professional feel to it.

Your LinkedIn profile is essentially a curriculum vitae/résumé that lists your current roles, skills and past experiences, etc., which is perfect information to target decision makers and candidates because you can easily identify key decision makers or people within an organisation.

I have a family friend who started a business selling tailor-made shirts online. On the surface it was a very consumer based business. But because he was able to analyse who his ideal customer was (males aged between 45-65 who earned over £70K/$100K a year), LinkedIn became one of his most valuable routes to market because he was able to target people who matched that description.

Moving away from LinkedIn, I remember reading a story of a guy who sold Russian mail order brides. After analysing his market, he realised that a very large percentage were male truck drivers. Knowing this meant he could tailor his marketing to speak directly to those people. His message used language that male truck drivers used, and he picked media that male truck drivers consumed.

Once you know your market inside out, you can tailor everything about your marketing to target those specific people. Not knowing your market is one of the fundamental mistakes which stops many Recruitment/Search Business owners from ever reaching their full potential.

Part 3:
Your LinkedIn
Message

*"So, a workmanlike definition of marketing is: getting the
right message to the right people via the right media."*
Dan Kennedy ~ The Ultimate Marketing Plan

Getting the right message in front of your audience

If you're like most Recruitment/Search Business owners, you're probably making the big mistake that's stopping your potential clients from ever buying from you, and you probably don't even know what that is. Well, let me share it with you. It's talking all about yourself and not identifying or solving your clients' problems.

You might have known that intellectually already; but I bet you'd forgotten it, or not properly grasped how important it is.

See, a typical website or marketing piece for a Recruitment/Search Business owners, starts off like this:

"Hi, welcome to my really boring website.

My name's (Name of Recruitment/Search Business owner) and that's really interesting, isn't it? I know you've got a problem in your business but before we get to that I want to tell you all about myself and how proud I am of being different.

We've been in business for longer than I can remember.

And you know what?

I love it! I love it so much I want to tell you all about my mission and all the cool things I want to do with my business.

Oh yes and on the next page I have photos of other members of the team..."

And so it goes. Utter crap. But I see it all the time and I bet you do too! The truth is, no matter how good a Recruitment/Search Business owner you are, no matter what experience you've got, no matter how long you've been in business, all your clients and candidates really care about is themselves, their problems and how to fix them. If you really want to get through to your potential clients and candidates and get them to work with you, then you first have to walk a mile in their shoes and demonstrate you've walked that mile.

I knew this intellectually too, but it didn't actually sink in until a mentor of mine, Jon McColloch, gave me his famous 'hemorrhoids' example. Just to be clear, his haemorrhoids aren't famous, but the example is one known by many.

It went something like this: imagine you've got hemorrhoids, and you're looking for a solution to the burning pain in your bum (I know it's not a nice thought, but there is a point to this, I promise). If you've ever suffered from haemorrhoids, then you'll know that all you really want is to get rid of the pain - that's all you care about.

So, when you're looking for a cure, you don't care how long the person selling you the ointment has been in business, you don't care about their mission statement either, you just want relief from the pain, and you want it quickly and effectively.

Long story short: No one wants your services. *They want the results your service provides.*

Many Recruitment/Search Business owners get this bit completely wrong and so lose out on leads, cash and clients. Remember the 'brand advertising' I spoke about in the last chapter, the one that focuses on the logo and company colours, which costs a fortune and only hopes to appeal to its target audience? Well, this is why it's so ineffective – the focus is all about the company – and not about the potential client. (And the problem they are having.)

Successful marketing comes down to getting your message right on every marketing piece you send out and every communication you have with a potential client, and also that it's done in a way that is measured and tested. Your LinkedIn profile and your LinkedIn interactions are no different.

Setting up a profile that *sells*

The basic functionality of LinkedIn is based around 'profiles'. These are unique identifiers that display the individual's information.

If you're familiar with LinkedIn, you may have noticed that it almost forces you to set up your profile in the style of Curriculum Vitae or Résumé.

You're asked for your name, date of birth, geographical location, current job title, past positions, education and qualifications. All great stuff if you're looking for a job or someone to employ. But it's also fantastic information when looking for your ideal client. (This is why having the profile of your target audience is critical – remember the FBI metaphor I used earlier?)

So when it comes to setting up your profile (and ultimately marketing your business), it's got to be different from all the others. When your ideal prospects hit your profile on LinkedIn, we want them to stop dead in their tracks and think to themselves, *"This Recruitment/Search Business is just who I've been looking for to solve my problem."*

In order for that to happen, there are a few vital things you must consider when setting up your profile.

Profile picture

When setting up your LinkedIn profile you have an option to add a picture that will be visible to your network and the people you're connected to. Earlier on in this chapter, I hammered home the point that your potential clients don't care about you, and all they want is a solution. This is true for the most part, but your profile picture is one of the few times where you (or the picture of you) becomes important to the client.

The three common mistakes people make when it comes to their profile picture;

The first is not having one at all. When setting up a LinkedIn profile from scratch, it's easy to skip this step thinking it's not important, especially if you don't have a good picture to hand. But your picture is **vital**. It doesn't matter what you look like, but it does matter that the prospect can put a face to the name.

And when I say, *"it doesn't matter what you look like"*, I mean as long as you're being true to yourself, it doesn't matter what you look like. I've had several clients who've been reluctant to put a picture of themselves on their LinkedIn profile because they believe it will stop them getting business. It's happened quite a few times for different reasons, but there are two examples that stand out in my head the most.

The first example is a black guy. He was worried that if his potential clients knew he was black, they wouldn't want to work with him. And the second example was a client who was a Muslim. Now he wasn't so concerned about his picture, but more concerned about displaying his real name because he thought some of his clients wouldn't like his ethical and religious beliefs.

My view on this is that yes, people may look at your picture and decide not to work with you on that basis. But do you really want to work with these people if that's how they judge who they work with? If someone is going to look at your picture and make a snap decision about whether you're qualified to help them solve their problem, then is this the kind of person you want to be attracting into your life?

Only you can answer that question, but my advice would be to avoid them at all costs. There are more than enough people who care about results more than they care about what you look like.

Be authentic, be true to yourself, and if someone doesn't like it, then you shouldn't want to work with them anyway.

That being said, people are automatically drawn to people they can identify with, so bear that in mind when choosing what image to use. I don't believe this to be vital, but it is certainly worth considering. If there's a particular image that represents authority in your niche, then you may want to include that in your picture.

For example, if you work within the medical sector, you may want to have a picture of you with a stethoscope or in a white coat. Or, if you work with lawyers, you may want to be wearing a suit or similar conservative clothing. What you don't want is a picture that is completely incongruent with what you are claiming to solve. A picture of a beautician with greasy hair and an unkempt appearance might not win over people looking for someone to help them with their appearance. I'm sure you get the gist. First impressions do matter, so take some time thinking about your picture and make sure it really represents you in the best possible way.

The second mistake that people make when it comes to their profile picture, or their whole LinkedIn account in general, is **having a company logo instead of a picture of themselves** – or having a profile that is only associated with their company.

For example, let's say John Smith owns a Recruitment/Search Business, called 'Smith Executive Search'. If John were making this mistake, the name on his profile would say 'Smith Executive Search' and the profile picture would be the company logo, when it should really display his name and a picture of himself (the face behind the personality). As I said before, this is one of the few areas your potential clients actually care about you; **people buy from people.** It's important they feel like they're having an interaction with an individual rather than a company.

The third mistake people make is not having a clear (or high enough resolution) picture. So maybe the picture they use has been taken with an old camera and the quality is not that great, or maybe it's a family picture with the kids and pet dog included. Having a picture that includes your family and pets can be appropriate, BUT in most cases, it's a good idea to have a photo of just yourself. Most smart phones have a camera with a really good resolution, and I'm sure you could find someone to help you take a great picture of yourself.

Remember, *people buy from people*. Social media users have been conditioned to look out for pictures, it's what our eyes are drawn to when we are browsing through these sites, and LinkedIn is no exception. This point will come up again when we look at the advertising system. But not having a picture on your profile makes people immediately suspicious.

Your name

I touched on this in the previous section with the *'Smith Executive Search'* example. But there's no harm in repeating the message to hammer the point home. Not having a name (or having your company name or not having your full name) is a big mistake. The name here needs to be congruent with the name you use on all your marketing messages, i.e., emails you send, how you sign off on letters, etc.

TIP: Your name is often the first thing people see when they come across your profile. As well as just putting your name, you can also use this area to put any extra information you may want your potential clients to know. For example, rather than just putting 'Terry Edwards', you could put 'Terry Edwards – Recruitment Client Attraction Expert'. I've seen people advise against this strategy, arguing that having anything other than your name in the name section can mean that when people search for you, you don't appear. It's a valid argument, but in 2013, my profile was listed by LinkedIn as 'within the top 1%' most viewed, so I must have done something right. This strategy wasn't solely responsible for this, but it clearly wasn't having any major negative impact either. Try it for yourself and see how you get on.

Your headline

Along with your profile picture and your name, your headline is one of the first things your potential clients and candidates will see when they come across your profile. The temptation here is to use the 'headline area' to put in your job title. (LinkedIn will encourage you to do this.) So when you look on the average LinkedIn profile that's exactly what you'll see.

Name: John Smith

Headline: CEO and Founder of Smith Executive Search

This is probably the right thing to do if you're looking for a job, but in our case we're looking for clients and candidates, and as we discussed earlier, all your clients and candidates care about are themselves, their problems and how to fix them. So instead of putting your job title, tell your ideal clients and candidates exactly what they want to hear.

"I help XXX to achieve XXXX."

Contact information

The contact information area of your profile is for all of your relevant contact details, and it will be visible to your connections. This includes your email, postal address, Skype name and contact telephone number. In addition, you can share your Twitter and WeChat names (if you have them), as well as your website details.

Now, your website area is really important, so let's focus for a moment on that. As I've said before, you're trying to get prospects *off LinkedIn and onto a media that you control,* and your website will play a big part in that.

Essentially, what you're trying to do with as many prospects and candidates as you can, is to get them onto your website, capturing their details so you can begin the dialogue with them outside of the LinkedIn platform.

When entering your web address into the website section, you have a few options to choose from. You can choose 'company website', 'personal website', 'blog', 'RSS Feed', 'Portfolio' or 'Other'. The natural reaction is to choose the option 'company website', which makes perfect sense because that's exactly what it is. The problem with choosing this option is that LinkedIn will then label that web address as 'Company Website', which isn't exactly compelling for your potential clients or candidates. If you're going to put your website on LinkedIn, you need to give your potential clients or candidate a real and clear reason to visit it.

If you choose the option that says 'Other' you get to choose the label yourself and therefore you can make it more compelling. For example, rather than saying 'Company Website' it could say *'How To Attract The Top Candidates*

In (Insert industry).' You've given the solution to your potential clients – by suggesting they will learn how to *'attract top candidates'.*

Your summary

The summary section is designed to summarise what you do now. Most people use it in the same way they would use it on a curriculum vitae/résumé and talk about what they're doing in their current job role or what sort of person they are.

For example, you'll see people waffle on about how much experience they have working in their current role and how good they are at their job, or how much they enjoy it. You may even see some Recruitment/Search Business owners talk about how long they've been in business and how good their service is.

Remember, your potential clients and candidates don't care!

All they want to know is how you can solve their problem.

I always see the best results when they use this area to drive visitors to their website or landing page. Don't forget, you are trying to **get people into your funnel of marketing.** You want to start a dialogue with them outside the LinkedIn platform.

For example, you could say something like.

"If you're a Hiring Manager and you have problems attracting top candidates who can do the job, visit my website at www.nameofwebsite.com and get a free report that reveals how to attract all the candidates you need without the headache."

Try and be as compelling as possible, and make it irresistible. Be benefit orientated and solve their biggest problem – you'll have them flocking to you in droves!

Your experience

The experience section of the profile is where you'll typically see information about past work experience. This is all background info, but make sure that your past experience is relevant to what you do *now*. Pay particular attention to your 'current' work experience. Make sure this section talks about exactly how you can help your clients.

Rather than putting information about your business (how long you've been operating, why you got into your niche), talk specifically about what problem you help your clients solve. This should be an extension on the 'summary' area of your profile.

As you can see, LinkedIn gives you some flexibility to play around with the layout of your profile. The standard structure is the same for everybody, but you do have the option to change the order in which things are displayed. I've found I get the best results when I put my summary first, then my experience, and so on. Feel free to play around with it yourself and do some testing. No changes are permanent so don't be afraid to test something new and see what results you get.

I can't predict the number of people who will visit your profile, but assuming you're putting into practice all of the strategies I'm explaining in this book, you'll naturally get more exposure to your ideal clients. Therefore, you might as well make sure that if and when they do get to your profile, you're giving them plenty of reasons to visit your website and engage with your message of solving their problems.

Part 4:

Utilising The Power of LinkedIn's Organic Traffic Source

"Friends Don't Always Come With Benefits."
~ Terry Edwards

Building your LinkedIn Connections

What are LinkedIn connections?

On LinkedIn, people who are part of your network are called 'connections'. If you're more familiar with Facebook or Twitter, this would be the equivalent of a friend or a follower. Unlike Facebook and Twitter, however, LinkedIn is more strict about who you add as a *connection*. They warn people who have no relationship against connecting with each other, and encourage connections to be someone you know well or who is a trusted business contact.

This limits you somewhat when it comes to using LinkedIn for marketing purposes, as a lot of the time you want to be generating business with people who *don't know you exist*. But there are ways to get around this, as I'll explain later.

Generally, the more connections you have, the bigger your network, and the bigger your network, the more people you're exposed too. However, having thousands of LinkedIn connections is not the Holy Grail.

What is *more important* is the number of connections you have with potential clients and candidates.

There are four main reasons why clients will never ever buy from you:

1. They have no NEED for your services.

2. They don't KNOW you.

3. They don't LIKE you.

4. They don't TRUST you.

So when you connect with a potential client or candidate it is the first part of the relationship.

I mentioned earlier, the goal of marketing on LinkedIn is to get your prospects off LinkedIn and onto a platform that you control. I've seen Recruitment/Search Business owners who have spent a lifetime on LinkedIn building their network of connections with it having no real or measurable impact on their business profits.

Why your LinkedIn network and connections are important

LinkedIn categorises each person in your network as an indicator of how closely they are connected to you. These are measured in tiers.

1st **Connection** - These are people who are directly connected to you. For example, if you connect with me on LinkedIn today, I will be your *'1st Connection'* and you will be my '1st Connection'. In terms of generating leads through LinkedIn organically, these are the low hanging fruit.

2nd Connection - These are people with whom you have a mutual connection. For example, if you connect with me on LinkedIn, all of my connections who you are not connected with will be your '2nd connections,' and vice versa.

3rd Connection – These are people who are connected to your '2nd Connections' and are considered part of your network.

Each person in your network can only fall into one of the above categories at any given time.

Group Members – People with whom you share a LinkedIn Group are also considered part of your network. People can be in your network solely because they are in the same group as you, or they can be in the same group as you and either a 1st, 2nd or 3rd tier connection.

A LinkedIn Group is a forum set up by an existing LinkedIn user, within LinkedIn, which others can join to partake in discussions and/or make new connections. They are generally specific and targeted to one particular area of interest.

People outside your network – anyone who doesn't fall into the categories above, will be classified as being outside of your network. These are people you haven't connected with and share no mutual connections with. In terms of generating leads through LinkedIn organically, these are the hardest people to reach.

You can still contact these people using LinkedIn's *'InMail'* feature or if you invest in one of the packages on offer from

LinkedIn, but these people are the hardest work.

The basic aim is to move the people who are outside your network to being inside your network (at least as a group member), and to move the group members to 3rd tier connections, the 3rd tier connections to 2nd tier connections and the 2nd tier to first.

These don't necessarily have to be sequential steps. For example, someone in your network can jump from being just a group member to a 1st tier connection without going through the other steps. But as a general rule, generating a lead from a 1st tier connection is 100 times easier. The profit in your LinkedIn campaigns will come predominately from your 1st tier connections, so the more people who fall into that category, the better.

It's not the number of connections you have, or the size of your network that is important, it's what you do with them.

Although LinkedIn connections aren't the be all and end all, assuming that you're targeting people who are in the market for buying what you sell, having more connections is better than having less.

And this is because the more people you have in your network, the more people are exposed to your message and what problem you help to solve. If the people you're connected to have the problem you're solution is designed for, then these are all potential clients.

Who to connect with

So the obvious question is: *"Who should I be connected*

with?" And I'll tell you in a moment. But it's amazing how many Recruitment/Search Business owners use LinkedIn to connect with old school friends, work colleagues, other Recruitment/Search Business owners and random people they were once associated with during their previous working careers.

I'm not saying forget about these people, but it's important to point out that this activity is *not marketing.* Connecting with these people will not generate leads, and it will not add profits to your business.

The only people you should be connecting with are your current clients; potential clients; potential candidates; candidates you have placed previously; potential joint venture partners and people you could form an alliance with. Occasionally you may have a friend or ex colleague that fits into these categories, but anyone else should be ignored.

Turning your connections into *leads*

So, understanding this principle, the real value of your LinkedIn connections now is what you do with them once they're in your network. There are a few things that I've found which have worked best for Recruitment/Search Business owners when it comes to profiting from LinkedIn connections, and these are detailed below.

Getting introductions

One of the biggest ways to profit from your LinkedIn connections is to use them to leverage relationships. Remember, birds of a feather flock together. So it's very likely that if you're connected to one of your ideal clients, then they will be connected to people who would also be ideal for you to work with.

For example, people that own legal firms are likely to be connected to other people that own legal firms...

People that work in finance are likely to be connected to other people that work in finance...

I could go on.

Usually, you would have no way of knowing who your client knows without asking them directly, and often someone who could potentially be important to you might slip your contacts mind when it comes to an introduction. But with LinkedIn, you can go and see who your connections are connected to. So now, instead of having to wait for an introduction (that might never happen), you can take the issue into your own hands and introduce yourself.

Let's use one of my clients as an example. Jim is a senior IT Recruiter within Sales. Typically it's Sales Directors and Managing Directors in the IT arena.

Now let's imagine that Jim is connected to one of his ideal clients on LinkedIn (we'll call him Bob). Now Bob is very likely to know other people who would be ideal for Jim's business, but probably wouldn't think to introduce them to him. After all, Bob is very busy and he's too caught up in trying to get business for himself, let alone introducing his connections to anyone else.

But this doesn't matter!

Using LinkedIn, Jim can go onto Bob's profile page and scroll through his connections that are displayed, looking for anyone that might be a right fit.

Immediately he has their name and job title, as well as a mutual connection, by means of Bob. So now Jim can reach out to anyone that fits his profile of an ideal customer, and introduce himself.

Here is an example of what Jim could say:

"Hey I see you're connected to Bob. I help IT Software companies add to their bottom line by attracting the leading sales professionals and I thought it would be worth me reaching out to you."

Sending Direct Messages

One of the big benefits of connecting with your ideal potential clients on LinkedIn is that once they become a 1st tier connection, you have the ability to send them a *direct private message* within LinkedIn. Remember I told you about how you should be trying to promote your connections to 1st tier? Well, this is one of the reasons why. There is one caveat to this strategy though, and that is: it can also be very time consuming, depending on how many connections you have. I used this feature more frequently in the early stages of my business building, but have used it much less since more automated and less time consuming alternatives have become available.

But if you did want to use this feature the option is there. What you can do is send your whole list of connections a message offering them a solution to the problem they're having.

The 3 step introduction method

One of the biggest complaints I get from Recruitment/Search Business owners when it comes to LinkedIn is that they have hundreds, and sometimes even thousands of 1st tier connections, all in their target market, but they're unable to turn those connections into **leads.**

An executive search firm shared with me a process that can be quickly copied and that's how I came up with the 'three step process'.

Step One: Convert your target into a 1st tier connection. Step one can happen when either you connect with someone directly, or they connect with you. As soon as you accept the request from them, or they accept the request from you and they become a 1st tier connection, step one is complete.

Step Two: Once they have become a 1st tier connection, send them a welcome message. You can either do this through the LinkedIn's built in messaging interface or, because you're now a 'connection', you can send them a direct email. I prefer to use the LinkedIn interface for this step as it seems like a quicker process. The welcome message is nothing complicated, it simply says something along the lines of,

"Hi,

Thank you for connecting and welcome to my network. It's really great to be part of yours.

I hope I can be a useful connection for you and please let me know if I can help you in any way."

The reason I recommend sending this welcome message is because it immediately makes you stand out from the crowd. If your target audience are anything like the majority of people on LinkedIn, they're likely to connect with multiple people every single week. For most people, once the connection has been made the relationship stops, there's no dialogue, no follow up - nothing. Sending them a welcome message immediately makes you different. You've taken the first step in initiating the dialogue and they're more likely to remember you.

Let's think about this in more detail. Imagine that on the day you connect with someone, five other people in the same market do exactly the same thing. Without sending a welcome message, you have no way of differentiating yourself from those other five people. Ordinarily, once the connection has been made, from a prospects point of view, you're forgotten pretty quickly. By sending the welcome message you take control of the situation and immediately stand out in the eyes of the potential client.

Step Three: The third and final step involves another message (either through the LinkedIn messaging interface or a direct email), but this time, instead of just welcoming them and introducing yourself, you make them an offer.

We'll talk more about irresistible offers in a later chapter, but basically you want to give them a solution to their problem in the hope that they'll raise their hand and express an interest.

Growing your group

In 'Part 5: LinkedIn Groups', I talk about the benefits of having your own LinkedIn Group.

One of the benefits of connecting with someone on LinkedIn is that once someone becomes a connection, it's easier to invite them to join your LinkedIn Group. Once they're in your group you can market to them again and again until they eventually buy from you. I'll cover exactly how later, but for now just open your mind to the possibility of starting your own group.

Facebook advertising

A point worth remembering about LinkedIn is that once someone becomes a connection, you gain access to his or her contact details. At this stage they've haven't opted in to receive any marketing emails from you, but don't make the mistake of thinking that their email address is useless. Facebook has an advertising system that allows you to specifically target users by their email address. This means that assuming the email address they've used on LinkedIn is also associated with a Facebook account, you can show your ad directly to these people right in the middle of their Facebook newsfeed. This is extremely powerful when you consider just how often people use Facebook. What it means is that once you've connected with someone on LinkedIn, you can then export their email address out of LinkedIn and import it into Facebook's targeting system.

Facebook will then show your ad about the problems you solve to that person, giving them the impression that you're everywhere. The more they see your message, the more likely you're going to be the one they think of when they're ready to buy. I prefer using this method over sending a direct message to them via LinkedIn.

Although you have to pay for the advertising on Facebook, it takes very little time in comparison to messaging people manually.

Also, you can use *Facebook Lookalike*.

What are Lookalike Audiences?

Lookalike Audiences are a way to reach new prospects who are likely to be interested in your business because they're similar to prospects and client's you care about.

When you use 'Custom Audience' you can choose to create a Lookalike Audience that targets people who are similar to one of your Potential Audience lists. You can create a Custom Audience using email addresses and/or phone numbers. Just keep in mind that your Custom Audiences must have at least 20 people in them.

You can create a Custom Audience with any of the following tools: Ads Manager, Ad creation, and Power Editor.

So if for example your target market is recruiting CIOs, when you connect with them on LinkedIn and then export their details and Import them into Facebook, you can then display your ad to other CIOs on Facebook.

As it is a Pay Per Click campaign, you only pay for ads if your potential client or candidate clicks on it.

How cool is that...?

As I said earlier, your prospect will never ever buy from you if:

1. They have no NEED for your services.

2. They don't KNOW you.

3. They don't LIKE you.

4. They don't TRUST you.

By displaying your ad to your potential prospect on Facebook, your prospect are getting to know you.

Twitter & your LinkedIn account

When you set up your LinkedIn account, you also have the option of adding your LinkedIn address as the two platforms are integrated.

This means you can follow your prospects and candidates on Twitter.

By the way, you should have *two separate twitter accounts,* one for clients and another for candidates, as the messages need to be relevant to your audience.

On LinkedIn there is a application called *Tweet* that helps you keep abreast of Twitter updates from your LinkedIn connections.

You can also identify and follow all your LinkedIn connections with the Tweets application.

LinkedIn *Influencer* and *Published Posts*

Relatively recently, LinkedIn added a 'Published Post' feature to its platform. This feature was previously only available to people LinkedIn considered a 'LinkedIn Influencer'.

The 'LinkedIn Influencer' title was given to approximately 500 professionals who were invited to publish on LinkedIn.

The list of influencers included Richard Branson, Bill Gates, Arianna Huffington, Guy Kawasaki and other people who are considered leaders in their industries. They published posts about broad topics of interest such as leadership, management, hiring and firing, and how to succeed.

Similar to a magazine with contributing editors, influencers had the role of developing content topics that LinkedIn believed to be relevant to members and would spark inspiring conversations.

A *'Published Post'* is essentially a blog that is held on the LinkedIn platform, rather than a private blogging site, but you no longer need to be considered as a *'LinkedIn Influencer'* to have access to this feature. They have made it available to everyone.

This is a powerful feature for several reasons. Firstly, every time you publish an article, all of your contacts get notified. This is no big deal in itself, but assuming you've included links driving people back to your website, it's a good way to generate additional leads from your connections. These posts will then become part of your LinkedIn profile, giving your prospects the opportunity to read them and hopefully visit your website (and opt into your list).

LinkedIn members who are not in your network can also follow you and get notified when you publish posts, so there is an additional opportunity to get some of those people to visit your website, too.

But remember, these 'posts' will only be profitable if you're using them to *drive visitors to your website*.

As it's a fairly new feature, I've only just started taking this option seriously. It's early days yet, but the results I'm getting and that of the Recruitment/Search Businesses I'm working with are very encouraging. It's a feature that if used correctly, can be extremely powerful. If you don't have the time to do this yourself, pay someone to do it for you!

A special gift from the 'Renegade Recruiter'

Join LinkedIn Lead Rush Supremacy (£197/$300 Value) FREE

Before you read any further, make sure you've signed up for LinkedIn Lead Rush Supremacy by visiting;

www.drewcoaching.com/LinkedIn-book

And get access to FREE tools and done for you templates, to help you increase your leads and increase your personal income.

www.drewcoaching.com/LinkedIn-book

Part 5:
LinkedIn Groups

"You are the average of the five people you spend the most time with." ~ Jim Rohn

Recently I sat down with a new friend that I met at a *'Marketing Mastermind'* group that I am a member of. We talked about what it takes to achieve your business goals. My friend is already a very accomplished marketing professional, and yet, there was lots more she wanted to do. One conclusion I kept coming back to in this talk was that a large amount of how successful you will be in life, all comes down to the people you spend time with.

Who are the people you spend time with?

It doesn't matter how smart you are. It doesn't matter how talented you are, which skills you have, where you were born, or which family you come from. The thing that really counts - if you want to be successful in your Recruitment/Search Business and in life - is the people you surround yourself with.

The people I spend time with

I took longer than most people to understand this concept. I clung onto relationships with people far too long. All of

75

them were great people, but I always knew these were not the type of people that were dying to be incredibly successful and willing to do what it takes to achieve their dreams. Some of these people had no understanding of business or marketing, yet were keen to give me their opinions on why what I was doing wouldn't work. Gradually I learnt to spend less and less time with them.

Today I'm a member of a *'Marketing Mastermind'* group that meets four times a year in Ireland, where members travel from all over the world to be there. Now I'm not sharing any of this to impress you, but to impress upon you the importance of the company you keep, as there will be a direct correlation to what you earn. (By the way, if you want information on *'Mastermind Groups'* for Recruitment /Search Business owners, drop me a line and I will get back to you.)

A word of warning: who you spend time with on LinkedIn will have an *impact on your earnings.*

The power of LinkedIn Groups

If LinkedIn is equivalent to a huge networking event, then *LinkedIn Groups* are like smaller breakout sessions that contain a more targeted demographic of who you're trying to reach. According to Wikipedia, at the time of writing this chapter, there are over 1,891,752 individual groups on LinkedIn.

That's not including the sub-groups. I'm not 100% sure of the legitimacy of that claim, Wikipedia is not exactly the most reliable source, but I do know there are lots and lots of groups on LinkedIn. Even if there is only half that number, it's worth looking at. Plus, remember that number will be growing every single day. So the chances are, by the time you're reading this book, there will be a few thousand more for you to consider.

There are groups for people with niche interests (such as what sports team they support) or unique hobbies, as well as local groups for particular cities or towns. There are groups aimed at people who work in a particular industry, as well as groups only for people with certain job titles. No matter what your target audience are into, you're sure to find something that meets their needs.

But why are the LinkedIn Groups so important?

A LinkedIn Group is great for bringing potential clients and candidates with common interests together. As a Recruitment/Search Business owner you should have a minimum of two groups, one for potential clients and one for candidates.

Remember, marketing is all about getting in front of your *target audience with the right message at the right time.* Doing your research (as you did at the beginning of the book) and knowing who your audience is, now pays dividends, because you should have a better idea of exactly what type of groups they'll be in.

Joining the right groups

Joining groups that are populated by your ideal clients allows you to get in front of them, so they can get to know, like and trust you, and ultimately become clients.

Unlike a traditional networking event where you have a limited amount of time to try and reach everyone in the room, with no guarantee of who is in your target audience, you can now stop wasting time speaking to someone who can be of no help to you or your business.

Networking in the groups on LinkedIn is completely the opposite. Firstly, (and I'm assuming you've joined a group aimed at your target audience) these people will be in your market, or have an interest in it. Secondly, even if they're not in your market, you can see exactly what they do before you speak to them; a luxury you don't get when meeting someone face to face.

And lastly, you have no time limits; once someone has joined a group they usually stay a member for the long term. Most people will join a group and never leave. This means you have plenty of time to cultivate a relationship with your potential client.

One of the mistakes Recruitment/Search Business owners make when it comes to LinkedIn Groups is joining the ones aimed *at them*. For example, they join a group where there are other Recruitment/Search Business owners.

This is fine if your purpose for joining the group is to network with peers and colleagues, but for the purpose of marketing, it would make more sense to join groups aimed at your *target audience*.

You can be a member of up to 50 different groups at any one time on LinkedIn, so it's OK to be in a few for personal benefit rather than business, but make sure the vast majority of them are filled with your target audience so you can profit from them.

How to profit from LinkedIn Groups

So, once you've joined all these LinkedIn Groups, how do you profit from them? Well, to remind you about what I said in one of the earlier chapters, the purpose of LinkedIn is to get them off LinkedIn's platform and move them onto a platform *you control*.

The best way to profit from this is to use the groups as LinkedIn intended, but with a slight twist. You should still ask and answer questions and start getting involved with discussions, but your aim should be to get as many prospects as you can into your sales funnel.

Most people who use the LinkedIn groups are using them as a forum to ask and answer questions. So to profit from them, you need to look at things in a different way. It's imperative that you have a strategy where you can measure your involvement and hopefully, results, otherwise, it's a pointless task.

At a very basic level, you must ensure that every contribution to a group discussion has a link driving visitors to your website or landing page. Even if that just means putting your web address in the signature of any post you publish. But even better, point them to a page that is relevant to whatever that particular discussion is about.

For example, if someone in your target market posts a question about '*Difficulty in finding top candidates*', you could then answer that question and include: "*if you want to find out more about this, there is a great report called 'Why Top Candidates Will Never Join Your Business'*" and it would include a specific link for a free eBook, www.linktolandingpage.com

This process would be repeated with any question people ask and send them to specific web pages, which answers that question. When they get to the page, the next step is to get their email information, so you can continue the dialogue with them outside of LinkedIn. (We'll talk more about what you should be saying and doing on your website to get these people to buy from you in a later chapter.)

As well as contributing to other people's discussions, you can also start your own. For example, a client based in the UK who recruited IT Contractors, has a group on LinkedIn just for IT Contractors in a specific field. She started a discussion *"What is the Most Ridiculous Question You Have been Asked in an Interview?"* Her group has about 3,400 members and she was inundated with responses. She took all the response and created another eBook called *'The 97 Questions That Will Stop the Top CIT Contractors from joining Your Business."*

She then started discussions in groups where there were hiring managers who recruited IT Contractors. At the end of her discussion she would say, *"if you're a hiring manager and you wish to get a competitive edge, get this free eBook and discover what you must never ever ask in an interview."*

Pretty smart!

On a side note, posting in groups will encourage more people to visit your profile organically. That's why the profile set up we looked at earlier becomes even more important.

Creating your own groups

As well as being able to join other people's groups on LinkedIn, you also have the option to create your own groups, too.

Creating your own group is a great way to position yourself as a leader in the sector you operate in. It allows you to create a herd of followers who are ready and willing to listen to your message.

One of the downsides of being in other people's groups is that you have to abide by their rules. All group owners have a different way of doing things. This isn't a big issue but it certainly can be frustrating. When you *own* the group, you can do what you like, however you like, and whenever you want to do it (within the rules set by LinkedIn). You can also choose what other people do and don't say too! It's your own private discussion forum and you control the dialogue. If one of your competitors says something you don't like, you can simply delete their comment or kick them out of the group altogether. If one of the group members annoys you for any reason, you don't have to put up with it. But more importantly, creating your own group allows you to build your own little community of prospects for you to profit from.

You can use your own group to start or participate in discussions and ask questions, with the added benefit of having no filter. You can pretty much say what you like and be as self-promotional as you want to be, without having to worry about stepping on anyone else's toes. This is in sharp contrast to using other people's groups for marketing, as you have to be aware of what you're saying so as not to upset the group owner in any way. (They can kick you off, remember!) When it's your own group, you're the only person you need to worry about.

Another big benefit of having your own group is that you have the ability to send *weekly group announcements*. A group announcement means that every single member of the group will get an email sent to their email inbox with your message. You can do this a maximum of once a week, but it's a good way to get a few extra leads without much additional effort.

Groups are also good for gauging what is topical in your niche. As you get to see the questions that are on peoples minds, this also provides inspiration for your eBooks and blogs.

Candidate Groups

As a Recruitment/Search Business owner you should be posting jobs in the group, as members of the group will get an email informing them of the job opportunities. Of course not everyone will be interested, but a few things will happen.

1. They will pass on those details to other candidates in the same field who may be interested.

2. It is an essential tool when sourcing candidates, and there is no cost or risk.

3. It helps position you as the *"Go to"* recruiter in that particular niche.

I used to work with a Medical Search firm in Australia and he had one of the largest groups on LinkedIn within that profession. When clients asked, *"why should I work with you?"* he would reply, *"Our company are the owners and managers of the largest groups on LinkedIn within our niche, which means you have immediate access to the top candidates in the industry to ensure your business objectives are achieved".* That was his USP.

The LinkedIn Groups offer all sorts of useful tools that you can take advantage of. You don't have to limit your group to interactions in the form of comments and questions.

Creating evergreen webinars on subjects like, *'Interview Techniques'* or, *'How To Attract Top Candidates'* is a great way to sell to many, rather than one to one which most recruiters do.

There is a Recruitment/Search Business owner in Canada that gets all of his business via monthly webinars that he promotes both in his group and other groups on LinkedIn. You can offer white papers and newsletters, and give them other information of high value.

Your group, your rules

As it is your group you should have well defined guidelines and rules for members of your group. These guidelines and rules generally provide users with community contacts, encourage them to post information in appropriate sections, and specify conduct that is acceptable and behaviour that can get them banned (spam or personal attacks on other group members, for example).

Making all members aware of the rules and guidelines also gives you a reference point when you have to handle a difficult situation with a member.

Be the leader of the group; it's important that once you have established your group, you need to lead the group effectively. It isn't enough to simply establish the group and then not participate. If you can't or don't want to lead the group for some reason, then you need to make sure that you delegate it to someone else. At the very least you need to participate in group discussions, but you should try to be more involved than that if possible.

Managing other people's groups

A number of my Recruitment/Search clients have also taken to managing other people's groups in their target market. There are some groups where the owner/manager is not always keeping on top of the admin so they have contacted the manager and asked them if they can become a joint manager of the group and help them manage it.

This has a number of benefits. As the manager of the group you decide who joins that group and who is rejected, so you can decide which of your competitors can join. The other benefits are of course that you manage the discussions that happen in that group and you can agree with the group owner to use the weekly announcement feature to promote yourself from time to time by offering a free eBook, report etc.

How to promote your LinkedIn Group

Your LinkedIn group will only really be beneficial when you have lots of people in it. So before you can start generating leads, you need to promote your group to get members to join.

Here are some ways that you can get target prospects into your group:

1. Organic growth

There are several strategies that have worked well for me when it comes to growing my LinkedIn group. I'll go through each of them in this section of the book, but the first is 'organic growth'. By organic growth, I mean any growth that occurs naturally. Of course, there are things you need to have in place, but once the seeds have been planted it happens without much additional work.

The first thing you need to consider is what to call the group. One of the mistakes people make when doing this step is naming it after their company or something that is associated with their business.

When you're brainstorming this, you should be considering, *"What are my target audience looking for?"* and then name the group accordingly. You do have the option to change the name once the group has been created so don't get too caught up on this one area. Ideally you want something that will come up in search results when your target audience are looking for the solution that you offer.

Apart from having the right group name, the rest of the organic growth happens as a by-product of all the other methods for growing your group. As you put to work the other strategies I'm sharing, people will join your group. The more people that are in and interacting with your group, the higher up it will appear in the search results and the more it will appear in people's news feeds. Generally, more exposure means more members.

2. Your current LinkedIn connections

The next thing to do is to get people to join your group by inviting your current LinkedIn connections. You can either do this by going through your connections one by one and sending them a personal message, or, when you own a group, you have the option to invite your own connections in bulk within the group management area. Sending a personal message to each one of your connections is usually more effective, but it takes more time to do this

3. Your email list

There is no real marketing benefit to doing this other than to gain more members to your group. You have the email address of these contacts, which is the main reason for having the group, so the main goal has already been achieved. But as I mentioned before, the more members a group has, the more exposure it gets.

More exposure means more people will join organically. Simply sending an email to your current email list with a link to your group is a great way to get more people to join.

4. Using the other LinkedIn groups

The fourth strategy you can use is promoting your group in the other groups aimed at your target audience. You can do this by either posting a discussion about your group or messaging the members of a certain group individually - or both if you choose. Whichever way you choose, be sure to approach it with caution. Some group owners might not like this, and you could get some negative feedback from them.

5. Outsource it

Lastly, you can outsource the whole process. Companies like www.spreadyourvoice.com offer a service to grow your group for you without you lifting a finger.

Growing your LinkedIn connections using groups

One of the side benefits of having your own LinkedIn Group is that you can use it to grow your connections. When you have your own group, it allows you to accelerate the growth of your network and gives you a better chance of converting the prospect into a lead and client.

When someone joins my group, I send them a message asking them to connect with me rather than sending an invitation out to them. As the owner of the group, you're in a position of authority - you'll get a really high uptake when using this method.

Part 6:
LinkedIn Advertising

"Nothing except the Treasury can make money
without advertising."
~ Thomas Babington Macaulay

What is LinkedIn advertising?

Before we get into the nuts and bolts of what the LinkedIn paid advertising system has to offer, there is something I have to address...

A lot of the Recruitment/Search Business owners I speak to have an issue with any form of marketing that is 'paid for', as they see it as an expense they can't afford.

I used to think exactly the same thing until I attended a marketing conference that changed my thinking on advertising 'costs'. The speaker asked the audience if anyone had a £20 note. A few people put their hands up, and he picked one of them and pulled them onto the stage. He then took the £20 note off the volunteer and handed them five £20 notes in exchange. He then said, *"If for every £20 you give me, I am willing to give you £100 in return, when would you stop giving me money?"*

Well, the answer is pretty obvious, *"never!"* You, me and anyone with half a brain would keep giving and giving until we stopped getting that kind of return. It's like a good investment, and that's exactly how you should view any money you spend on marketing. If you pay for advertising, then you should get that money back in the form of a paying client. The sooner you grasp that concept the better!

LinkedIn, like any other form of marketing, should be viewed as an investment - you pay for the responses you get - but you get it back in the form of paying clients. It's not rocket science; it's fairly straightforward and easy to do as long as you remember the golden rule. *Get people off LinkedIn and onto a media that you control.*

One of the major benefits of LinkedIn advertising (and others of its kind) is that it's done on a 'pay per click' basis. This means your ads are displayed to users based on what you've told LinkedIn about your ideal client, with no cost for your ad to be displayed, until someone clicks on your ad. Hence the term: 'Pay Per Click'. (PPC)

It's *pay per response* marketing. It's a bit like running a television commercial, but rather than it going out to the whole viewing public, it only goes out to people you want to reach, and even then you don't pay for it until the viewer decides that they're interested enough to call or visit your website.

This means that if your ads aren't working, then you don't pay a thing, eliminating the risk associated with other forms of advertising.

You'll often hear people say they've tried PPC but it didn't work for them. Often it's because they're getting one of the four steps wrong, rather than PPC itself.

This isn't just on LinkedIn either, I hear people say this about almost any form of paid advertising.

Here is the ad cycle in four main stages.

1. You select what demographic of people you want your ad to be displayed to.

2. Once your ad is displayed, the ones who are interested will click on it and visit your website.

3. You then use your website to get these people off LinkedIn and onto a media that you control (like email for example).

4. You then use the media(s) that you control to convert these people into a client.

So even if you've tried it and it didn't work for you, that doesn't mean it can't be fixed. We'll look at each of these stages in more detail as we progress though this section of the book.

Why is it so powerful?

When you sign up to have a LinkedIn account, part of the process involves giving LinkedIn all sorts of personal but relevant information about yourself.

LinkedIn knows your name, date of birth, geographical location, you current and previous job titles, the current and previous companies you've worked for and how long you were at those companies for.

It also knows the size of the company you own and how many people you employ, including what industry your company operates in. It also asks for the skills you have acquired during your employment; pretty much any skill is encouraged to be declared. You're also asked for a personal residential address, an email address and telephone numbers... the list is almost endless.

Then, once you've got your profile built and you start actively using LinkedIn, it gets to know what groups you've joined, what types of people you're connected to, what profiles you visit and what company pages you follow. I could go on...

LinkedIn is essentially a massive detailed database of potential clients. It knows things about them that many other platforms will never know and, better yet, it's designed to keep people coming back again and again.

But what does that mean to you? Well, LinkedIn advertising essentially lets you target your ideal clients using all the detailed information LinkedIn has got.

Geographically, you can target people who live on a particular continent, in a particular country, or even a particular city, by pinpointing users by their postcode. When it comes to targeting by company, you can pinpoint people by name, a particular industry, or by size. You can target people who have specific job titles, or by the seniority of their role. You can target people by what school they attended or by what subject they studied. You can even handpick people that have a particular degree! You can target people by the skills they have, what LinkedIn groups they are in, their age and even their gender if you want to. And you can use various combinations of the above to find your ideal client. Its laser focused targeting to a degree that most forms of media can't even touch.

If LinkedIn is a media that your market uses, even if it's only on a small scale, it's set up for you to reach them, get their attention, generate their interest and turn them into someone who wants to buy your services.

Types of ads

When it comes to paid advertising on LinkedIn, there are two possible routes you can go down. Both have their pros and cons, and we'll look at them shortly.

But the important thing is to test both in your business and see what works best. Don't assume anything, just test and let the market tell you. You may be surprised at what you find. Also, because the two types of campaign display their ads in different places, there is no reason why you couldn't do both at the same time. Again, the same rules apply; test and see what works best for you.

There are, in my view, a few negative points to the LinkedIn advertising system that I must point out. The first of which is the lack of attention the bigwigs at LinkedIn appear to give it in comparison to other areas of the site. As I mentioned earlier, LinkedIn is constantly making changes to its platform. There have been countless changes since I first opened an account and I expect that to continue as it looks for ways to improve. But comparatively, the advertising system has changed very little. When it was first launched it was way ahead of its time; there was no other way to really tightly target a group of people online. Since then, however, other platforms have entered the market and are seemingly overtaking LinkedIn. The two that spring to mind are Facebook and Twitter. In a short time both these platforms have offered an advertising system to the mainstream.

They've made improvement after improvement to make it better, more effective and easier for advertisers like you and I to profit from. I can't say the same for LinkedIn.

I suspect there are several reasons for this, one of which is that advertisers are not their main revenue stream, or at least not their only revenue stream. For others, such as Facebook, Twitter and Google (to an extent), the money they get from ads is their main source of income. For LinkedIn, it's different. It has paid profiles for people who are looking for jobs; for sales professionals looking for leads; for recruitment companies looking for employees, as well as the display ads we're talking about, and premium display ads aimed at the big corporate companies. They have multiple streams of revenue, which makes them somewhat lazy in their approach to make any improvements.

I think they're missing out big time, because even a very small tweak - like making the ads bigger and more prominent - could make a massive difference.

Small changes like that would make ads more effective, which could mean more businesses wanting to advertise. And if more small businesses used the advertising system, there would be more competition for ad space, which means they could charge more and make more profit. Perhaps one day in the future things will change, but for now we'll just have to accept it as it is.

I once interviewed someone from LinkedIn's sales department for my 'Recruiters LinkedIn Leadrush' product. I wanted to include her tips on how to use LinkedIn as a free bonus, which seemed like a good idea at the time. But during the interview, it became clear that she didn't really know the advertising system existed. And that's not a criticism of her, but it just goes to show what little priority it gets.

Saying that, to date, it still provides me with the best quality leads above any online advertising I have ever done! So although it could be greatly improved, it is still amongst the best!

Paid display ads

The first type of campaign you can create is *'paid display advertising'*. This is the type of ad you may be more familiar with, as it's been around for the longest.

It also happens to be the type of ad that works best in my business, and all the Recruitment/Search Business owner clients I've worked closely with.

Saying that, as I mentioned previously, that does not necessarily mean it will be the same for you. You should test it and find out for yourself. These ads are displayed in several places: along the top of the home page once you've logged onto LinkedIn and on the top right hand side of the home page. See figure 1 on the following page. You may also find them on the bottom right hand side on the home page, and when you're viewing someone's profile.

With these ads, you have the option of just text ads, an image plus text ad and also video ads. The image plus text ads have always worked best for me, but you should test all options. We'll look in more detail at what makes an effective ad later on in this chapter.

Figure 1 - Paid display ad

Sponsored content

The second type of campaign you can create is a '*sponsored content*' campaign.

This type of campaign was introduced more recently by LinkedIn and involves your ad being displayed on your activity feed when you click on the homepage of LinkedIn whilst logged on.

If you're familiar with Facebook, your LinkedIn activity would be the equivalent of your Facebook 'news feed', and basically shows a timeline of activity based on your connections.

See figure 2 on the following page.

There are pros and cons for both types of campaign but, as I mentioned earlier, the only way to find out which one works best for you is to test them and measure the results.

Figure 2 - Sponsored content

Targeting

Who's my ad being shown to?

As I mentioned previously, who your ad is being displayed to is part one of the four stages associated with LinkedIn advertising. Here is where knowing *all about your target market is vital* – and it becomes even more important when you're paying for it.

Often, people get their targeting really wrong. They're too broad with who it is they want their ad to be displayed to, and pay a price in diminished results.

One of the most common mistakes I see is **not targeting the decision maker**. You should only be targeting people who have the authority to make the buying decision.

And this goes for all of your marketing. People often make the mistake of thinking that the goal is to show their ad to as many people as possible, but they're missing the point.

Your audience needs to be as big as possible, but it's crucial for it to be as *targeted* as possible, especially in the early stages. Quality is a lot more important than quantity. It's much better to have a really targeted list of one thousand people than it is to have a huge list of one hundred thousand people. Even if you have a big audience, it's better to run several smaller campaigns targeting mini- segments of that audience.

So, for example, a client who is an IT Recruiter for online bricks and mortar retailers in both the UK and USA, they would target CIOs HR Directors and VP HR in the UK, who work for retailers online and offline.

They could then set up another ad campaign targeting CIOs HR Directors and VP HR in the USA.

Each of these campaigns would have different ads; I'd use slightly different language to better craft a message which meets that particular demographics' needs, and I would get better results for doing so.

Don't sacrifice quantity for quality. The more targeted the better.

You only pay when someone clicks on your ad, so in theory, all that matters is the number of clicks you get rather than the number of people who see your ad. This is true, but showing an ad to more people than you need to is increasing the risk of wastage. By wastage I mean people who click on your ad who have no intention of buying. This happens to some extent anyway, even with a targeted audience, but we want to avoid it where possible. People clicking on your ad who are not in your target market is just a waste of money.

On the other end of the scale, if your ad is being displayed to people who have no intention of buying and they don't click, LinkedIn will punish you for it. Better performing ads get rewarded by being displayed more often and being displayed more often means more clicks, and more clicks means more leads. If your ad is being displayed to too many people who aren't interested, LinkedIn will assume it's a bad ad and it will be displayed less, or you'll have to pay more to have it displayed.

The targeting of your ad is just as important as any of the other four elements discussed earlier. Get it wrong and your ads won't work at all, or at least they won't be as effective as they can be.

Getting people to click on your ad

No matter what type of campaign you choose to run, the end goal should always be the same; to get prospects or candidates to respond by clicking a link that drives them back to your website and landing pages.

There are a few basic principles you should follow if you want to get the highest number of people clicking on your ad as possible. These are as follows:

Picture

Both the *sponsored updates* and the *paid ad* campaign types give you the option to display a picture with your ad. If you're displaying your ad to people who would know you, then you may want to test by using a picture of yourself.

Headline

A *'sponsored update'* campaign type doesn't give you a specific area as such to insert a headline, but essentially, the first text you type in will perform as the 'headline'. You want to use this to get the reader's attention and encourage them to read further.

Body copy

The body copy is there to give the reader a bit more detail on what it is you're offering, with the goal of getting them to click on the ad. If a prospect is reading this part, then you've got their attention with the picture, and their interest with the headline.

How much space you get and the size of the picture depends on what type of ad you create (sponsored update or display ad). You typically get more space to write a longer headline and body copy with a sponsored content ad. I recommend using all the space you have available to you, just make it relevant to your offer.

In short, the picture is to grab the prospect's attention, the headline is to develop their interest and the body copy is designed to create desire and get the prospect to actually click on the ad.

Running your ads

After you've launched your campaign, there are a few things you need to be aware of in order to get the best possible results. There are several things to consider when monitoring the effectiveness of any given ad in a particular campaign.

Figure 3 - Ad campaign reports

Reporting for your campaign is broken down into five main columns, as shown above in figure 3.

1. Clicks

2. Impressions

3. Click Through Rate (CTR)

4. Average Cost Per Click (CPC)

5. Total Value

Clicks

This refers to how many times someone in your target audience has clicked on that particular ad in your campaign.

Impressions

This refers to the number of times your ad has been displayed to the people your targeting with a particular campaign.

Click Through Rate (CTR)

This is the number of clicks you've received divided by the number of impressions that particular ad has had. As a general rule, the higher the CTR the better the ad is performing.

Average Cost Per Click (Avg. CPC)

The Average CPC refers to the average cost *per click*.

Total Value

This shows how much money has been spent on any particular ad, or collective ads in any given campaign. I touched on it earlier, the return on investment is far more important than how much you've actually spent.

Testing and Measuring

The real key to creating a successful LinkedIn advertising campaigning is to 'split test'. Usually, whatever you measure can then be improved. Once your campaign has started, keep an eye on how it's performing, and tweak and optimise your ads in order to get the best possible return.

A special gift from the 'Renegade Recruiter'

Join LinkedIn Lead Rush Supremacy (£197/$300 Value) FREE

Before you read any further, make sure you've signed up for LinkedIn Lead Rush Supremacy by visiting;

www.drewcoaching.com/LinkedIn-book

And get access to FREE tools and done for you templates, to help you increase your leads and increase your personal income.

www.drewcoaching.com/LinkedIn-book

Part 7: Irresistible Offers: Getting Your Potential Clients to Raise Their Hands

"There are basically two types of offers. There is an offer requesting purchase. There is also the lead generation offer, asking only for the person to, in effect, raise their hand, to identify and register themselves as having an interest in a certain subject matter and information - or goods or services - and invite further communication from you." Dan Kennedy ~ No B.S. Direct Marketing

There is no one part of the LinkedIn system that is more important than another. They are all equally important to the entire process. If one small area isn't working properly or working to the best of its ability, the whole system suffers...

With that being said, your *'irresistible offer'* – which is a relatively small part of the LinkedIn jigsaw – is still crucial, and you'd be a fool to ignore it as you could miss out on thousands of untapped profits and business revenues.

Your offer is designed to get a new prospect to step forward, indicating a need for your service and giving you permission to sell to them. This is often done by creating and offering free *'information of relevance'* to what you sell, which hopefully is of interest to the prospect.

Most Recruitment/Search Business owners have a version of this concept in the shape of a free consultation. This may seem like an irresistible offer to you, but from the client's point of view, all they really hear is:

"I have to spend an hour, maybe two with this person I don't really know that well, who's probably going to ask me all sorts of personal questions about my business, who might not even be able to help me because my problem is unique, and who at the end of it is going to try to sell to me..."

All of a sudden, your no risk irresistible offer for a free consultation turns into the client's worst nightmare.

Let's imagine you're an IT Search firm and your average fee is £20k/$30k. Rather than trying to get them to meet with you right from the off, what you could offer is a free eBook called: *'7 Questions To Ask an IT Search Firm Before You Spend Any Money With Them.'*

This offer works hand in hand with the web page you're driving people to. It's where the 'thing' that they're giving you their contact information in exchange for - it's the 'thing' that gets their juices flowing, the 'thing' they can't leave your webpage without getting - it's irresistible! Hence the name.

What you're essentially trying to do is identify the people who have the problem your services solve, by offering them a *straight out of the box solution*. This can come in many forms and there is really no right or wrong answer, it all depends on what works for your potential client.

It can be a book (either hard copy or digital), a video, or a series of videos (either hard copy or physical form), a free report, a webinar, etc.

You have lots of options. The only rule is it needs to be *irresistible' in the eyes of your potential clients.* For best results, it needs to contain information that they would ordinarily consider paying for, or content that wouldn't be available to them. But instead of asking them to pay for it, you're asking them to exchange their email address, or even their name, phone number and postal address so that you can follow up with them in multiple ways.

This is the basic principle to having a *lead conversion model,* rather than trying to get a sale off a complete stranger straight off the bat. Instead, you're simply trying to find the people who are interested in solving a certain problem so that you can put all of your time and effort into converting them into a client.

In the old days, before this was possible, you would have been forced to jump into the hard sell with prospects that may not even have been interested in whatever it was you had to sell. With this model, you're eliminating the people that aren't interested right from the beginning of the process. This strategy should form the **backbone of every online marketing campaign you run.**

1. Prospect responds to ad.

2. Prospect visits webpage.

3. Prospect requests *irresistible offer* in exchange for name and email address.

4. Prospect is followed up with emails and nurtured.

5. Take the relationship to the next level (contact via phone to establish needs)

6. Arrange meeting (face to face or on the phone)

7. Sale is made.

8. Deposit revenue into the bank.

9. Repeat steps 1 to 9.

It's a simple process, but it works!

A lot of my colleagues have used the dating analogy when trying to explain this to business owners.

The dating analogy

Would you do it on the first date?

Let me explain.

When you meet your ideal partner, even if it's *'love at first sight,'* I very much doubt you would propose on the first date. You are almost certainly going to get a NO! and rightly so.

Before anyone would make such a commitment, they would need to develop a relationship with them first. The same applies to your ideal client!

In order to get the best results from your marketing on LinkedIn (or otherwise), you need to be nurturing and developing the relationship you have with potential prospects over time, just like you would if you were courting someone. You build trust over time, and allow the relationship to flourish. You want your potential clients to feel comfortable handing over their details and 'commit' by buying your services.

You see, a large percentage of what influences someone to buy, is the relationship they have with you. They need to trust that what you offer will get them the results they want, and they need to know that you are the right person to deliver them.

The role of the irresistible offer is to begin that relationship.

Part 8:
How to Convert Your Prospects into Clients

"Half the money I spend on advertising is wasted;
the trouble is I don't know which half."
~ John Wanamaker

Converting the people that click on your ad and turning them into leads

This, in my opinion, is where the majority of Recruitment/Search Business owners get it wrong when it comes to online marketing: the conversion part of the process.

In my experience, whenever I've spoken to a Recruitment/ Search Business owner who complains that their online marketing isn't as effective as it could be, it's usually down to what they're saying or doing on their web page.

Just to be clear, the purpose of an ad on LinkedIn is to get the prospect to click on it.

Once the ad is clicked, the prospect is driven back to a web page. What you say and do on that web page will determine whether this person becomes a lead or just a wasted opportunity.

The same rules apply when talking about the organic LinkedIn marketing we discussed earlier. Remember, the goal is to get prospects off LinkedIn and onto a platform that you control. That's where your web page comes in.

What is web conversion?

On a typical website, only 1% of visitors take any action at all. This means that for every 100 people you get to your website, only 1 of them will pick up the phone and call you, buy from you or take the action you want them to take.

One of the things you need to be constantly improving with online marketing, especially when you're paying for ads, is your web conversion. You want as many people as possible to convert into a lead.

Passing the 8 second test: What your web designer won't tell you!

If you think about the way you 'surf' the web, you quickly go from one website to another, never really staying too long and often never returning to the same site more than once.

In fact, 50% of people who visit any given website will make the decision to leave it within just 8 seconds.

You need to interrupt that pattern and get your prospects to stay on your website and take the action you want them to take.

And you do that by...*The lead conversion model*

The purpose of your site is not to get people to buy from you immediately. Even if you get everything right up to this stage, it's very unlikely someone is going to click on one of your LinkedIn ads, land on your website and immediately get the credit card out and buy. It does happen, but it's very rare. In the previous chapter, I used the dating analogy to describe why this doesn't happen.

You will get much better results when you switch from using your website to sell and instead use it to promote your 'irresistible offer', and begin a relationship with your visitor.

What you are essentially saying is this...

"You don't know me yet, but I think I have something that's going to solve the problem you're having. If this irresistible offer is of interest to you, then please let me know by giving me your name and your email address. I'll then give you access to the irresistible offer and keep in contact with you about more ways you can solve the problem you're having."

Although this book is focused around LinkedIn, I felt it was really important to have at least one section dedicated to your website and web pages. Because, as I mentioned earlier, your chief goal is to get people off LinkedIn and onto a platform you control, such as email and direct mail, so you can continue the dialogue with them outside of the LinkedIn platform. Your website will play a huge part in that and I've mentioned this earlier, in part 2 and 3.

Without exception, in all of the strategies we've looked at so far, the goal has been to get your prospects off LinkedIn and onto a platform you control. Your website is the perfect gateway to do this. On your LinkedIn profile, I gave you an example of how I used my website (renamed as the solution) as a place to visit. And I've spoken about the *'irresistible offer'* being some form of information – which in turn is delivered by giving you their details – all of which is conducted from your web page. So, you can see how your web pages are a vital component in ensuring your LinkedIn campaigns are successful.

If you're like most of the Recruitment/Search Business owners I speak to, you probably already have a website and know the importance of having an online presence.

The problem is, you haven't yet figured out how to make it work for you in your business.

Not long ago, we conducted a survey of over 6000 Recruitment/Search Business owners from around the world. We discovered that more than 99% of the people we asked were either not generating any online leads at all, or weren't generating as many as they would like.

In this section of the book, we'll be looking at what the top 1% of Recruitment/Search Business owners (who generate all the leads they can handle online) do differently, and how you can do the same.

How the top 1% of Recruitment and Search Business owners use the internet differently

For the top 1% of Recruitment/Search Business owners their website is not just an information highway, it's a client attraction tool!

A client attraction tool that can be utilised 24 hours a day, 7 days a week, and 365 days per year. They don't care about having a fancy website with all the bells and whistles, all they care about is whether or not their website does what it's supposed to do.

Your burning question should be, *"how do I do that?"*

How do the top 1% of Recruitment/Search Business owners use their website to attract clients?

What are the implications for your personal income and your family security if you don't do this?

In a minute, you are about to get the answers to these questions. But first, it's important you understand the real purpose of all your online activity.

The purpose of any Internet marketing campaign, or anything you do online, comes down to two core principles:

1. Increase the number of potential clients who visit your website(s).

2. Increase the percentage of website visitors who convert into leads.

If any activity you engage in online doesn't do either of those things, then you're wasting your time.

Firstly, you must STOP any activity that doesn't do these things immediately: such as, using your website as an online brochure to tell potential clients all about YOU, or pointless tweets and Facebook updates that are of no interest to your potential clients.

Everything we've looked at so far covers the first of the two core principles. It's vital you have the second one covered too.

Part 9:
The Missing Link

*"Not following up with your leads is as crazy
as filling up your bathtub without first putting
the plug in the drain." ~ Anonymous*

Any form of Internet marketing doesn't just stop with your website, and the same applies to LinkedIn. A lot of Recruitment/Search Business owners neglect *following up* with prospects properly, and are missing out on thousands of pounds in business revenue and profits

The power of email follow up

In the last chapter, we looked at the principle of giving something of value away free in order to get contact details, which we then use to develop a relationship with a potential client (by using email and other marketing methods).

Your website and *'irresistible offer'* are there to start the relationship. The selling and the additional business profits actually happen after that point.

In order for that lead to want to buy from you, you need to cultivate that relationship and that's where *email marketing comes in.*

If you're not emailing your prospects regularly, you're almost certainly losing out on potential clients.

I'm yet to meet a single person or hear a single story where someone has sent more emails, but made less money. When we first started sending emails, we were sending one email per week, if that. And we were still sending more than most people in our industry. Today, we'll send an email almost every day, and if you're on my email list you'll know that to be true.

To most people that sounds like too much, but I'll repeat what I said earlier...

I'm yet to meet a single person or hear a single story where someone has sent more emails, but made less money.

I can understand that you may be uncomfortable with this idea; I was too. But don't form an opinion without **testing** it in your own business first. More to the point, don't listen to anyone else's opinion without testing it in your own business first, either. All I can tell you for certain is that *the more emails we send, the more money we make.* Without exception.

Taking things offline

No matter how well online marketing is working for you, one of the biggest mistakes you can make is to become solely dependent on the internet. It's not safe for any Recruitment/Search Business owner to have all of his or her eggs in one basket, no matter how profitable that 'basket' may be.

Combine your online follow up with one offline communication as well. Some people will buy off the back of your online communication, but some of your prospects will need more.

Nurturing a lead until they buy

However you choose to do it, it's all about relentless follow up. I have a mantra that I stick by when it comes to following up leads. *"Keep going until they either buy, die or say goodbye..."*

My theory is, most kids have this step just about mastered by the age of two.

Don't believe me?

I remember my youngest when he was two-years-old. He struggled to walk in a straight line most of the time, he was also probably amongst the top five messiest eaters in the world and had the attention span of... well, a two year old!

But anyone that has been fortunate enough to spend even a short amount of time with a two year old will know how tenacious they are, and masters of the relentless follow up! Take the question, *"Can I have some chocolate?"*

A typical two year old will ask and ask for their favourite sweet snack until eventually you give in. The same approach should be taken with your follow up. It's relentless, it never stops, or sleeps, until the prospect is ready to *buy, die or say goodbye..*

Did you know that only **2% of your prospects make a buying decision after the first contact?** So, if you're like most Recruitment/Search Business owners I deal with, and you don't follow up enough, you're leaving *98% of your business profits on the table for someone else to take.*

How long can you afford to keep doing that?

Therefore, the next step in this process is all about following up with your prospects, creating a second 'irresistible offer' that's linked to whatever step you want the prospect to take next.

For example, here is where you *may* want to offer the chance of a free one-on-one consultation with you.

At this stage of the process they know who you are, you know they have a problem and they know you have some expertise when it comes to solving it. There is a lot less risk from the potential client's point of view at this stage compared to the example I gave you earlier.

Why you need to be relentless at following up

I touched on the importance of follow up in order to get your prospects to know, like and trust you, but let's take a slightly different look at the reasons why people don't respond, even when they DO like and trust you.

Here are just a few reasons why your most seasoned and loyal followers might not respond immediately, and why you need to keep reminding them:

1. They didn't get your message the last time.

2. They got it, but didn't read it.

3. They were in a bad mood.

4. Last week they didn't need your services, but this week they do.

See, there are LOTS of reasons why they didn't say "yes" at the time, that have absolutely nothing to do with them saying "no".

I can think of many occasions where a potential client has initially reached out to me, saying something like, *"thank you for your offer, but I'm happy without any extra help and support"*, only to come back a few weeks or months later (after receiving more information from me), saying something along the lines of, *"actually, I've decided to try your service, as I really like your approach."*

It happens all the time, and it's all thanks to the consistent follow up process.

One of my 'Elite' clients was like most of my new clients, reluctant to email more frequently. His concern was, *"What if I piss them off with my relentless marketing?"* (By the way he is right, some prospects will not like it and they will unsubscribe.) But so what? You can still call them if you so wish.

Also what is the point of having a list of 2000 potential clients and emailing them say once a month? In a year your prospects will get 12 emails from you, yet your direct competitors emails five times a week, so in a year the same prospects get 150 emails from them. Who do you think your prospects are going to remember when they have a need for a Recruitment/Search Business?

And THIS is just another reason why you shouldn't just send random marketing pieces, make a random cold call or offer patchy promotions occasionally and then call it a day. THIS is why we have multi-step, multimedia campaigns. Because it's true, some people respond better to different mediums, such as email or direct mail, and others respond better to a personal phone call.

Can I use the above techniques to find candidates too?

A resounding *yes* is the answer.

LinkedIn can be a gold mine if you're recruiting. Where else can you find more than 300 million business professionals in one place prominently displaying their job experience, skills, education, recommendations, and expertise?

It's estimated that 74% of all employed professionals are willing to listen to you if you have an interesting opportunity for them.

And here is the key point; *you have to make the opportunity interesting to them.*

You sending an 'In mail' with the usual BS that they get from every other Recruitment/Search Business will not cut it.

With 74% of all employed professionals willing to listen to your job opportunity, how can you find these candidates? And when you do find them, how can you narrow your search to approach the very best candidates?

Let's use an example to explain how the process works.

Let's say you are looking for a CIO to implement and oversee quality IT systems for a major online retailer company. Your job requirements are:

1. Previous experience in IT Retail.

2. Significant knowledge on the latest online shopping and online marketing software and techniques.

3. Excellent communicator and team player with the ability to proactively address board members and finish projects on time and to budget.

With these requirements, you can go to the LinkedIn *Advanced Search* feature and find some candidates.

Here's how: On the right side of your LinkedIn toolbar or menu, make sure you're set to *People Search*. Click on the *Advanced* link, which is next to the magnifying glass to the right of the search box. For this search, we want to modify the parameters as follows:

1. In the Title field, enter *"CIO"* if you're looking for someone who currently holds that position or held that position in the past. You can change the drop down to choose Current or Past.

2. Change the Industries from *All Industries* to just **Retail and Online Retail.**

3. Change *Seniority Level* to **Director**. (This option is available only to LinkedIn Premium members.)

4. Leave all the other options at their default settings.

If you take a look at the preliminary search results, you'll most likely see hundreds of directors in that field. Not all of these people are looking for a job, but I bet at least a few of them would be open to listening to a new opportunity sounded interesting.

Before you start reaching out to some of the candidates you find with your first search, narrow your search a bit to see if you can find better qualified candidates.

The next step is to start looking at the profiles of these prospects to see if they're actively looking for work, which could be displayed in their profile headline. You can also look near the bottom of their profile where it says *'Advice for contacting name'* and see what it says. If it says Career opportunities, you know you're onto a winner.

N.B. You can add or remove the reasons for people to

contact you in your Profile Settings. Select Edit Profile under the Profile tab on the LinkedIn menu, and scroll down the page until you come to the *"Contact name for"* section and Edit to change your preferences.

If your search returns some LinkedIn members who are interested in Career Opportunities, you have a few options:

1. If you have a paid account you can send them an InMail to introduce yourself. Don't start out by asking them if they're looking for a new position or you may scare them away—even though their profiles say they're interested. Tell them you came across their profile on LinkedIn and saw something that caught your attention. Find something unique, like an award they won, interesting certifications, schools they attended, etc. You can ask them about these things or congratulate them. Try to establish a relationship so you can get to know them and see if they're a fit for your opportunity. If you mention things you have in common, they'll be more likely to respond to you. You could offer them an EBook such as '25 *Top Interview Question For CIOs That If You Can Answer Well, Will Guarantees A Job Offer.'*

2. Find groups they belong to and join that group, so you can reach out to them by sending them a message. At the beginning of your message, state that you both belong to the same group and you thought they may be interested in an opportunity that you're currently working on. As I mentioned earlier, joining groups where your audience are members and participating in discussions means when you reach out to candidates they know of you.

If they see your name regularly in the forum, they're more likely to respond to your messages even if they've never corresponded with you in the past.

3. If they're a second tier connection of yours, find out who in your network is a first tier connection between you and ask for an introduction. You can also ask your first tier connection what they think of that person to help determine if they would be a good fit for the opportunity that you're working on.

4. If they are part of the *LinkedIn OpenLink Network,* you can send them a regular message without having to use an InMail. People who are members of the OpenLink Network are open to people reaching out to them with job opportunities.

There's a word that sends me into a cold sweat. It's called *'networking.'* Many years ago, when I owned my own Search Business, I used to attend networking events at least three times a week.

I was told that the way to get business is through relationships, and by attending local networking events I would have lots of relationships and therefore lots of business. Sadly *not a single one of those lavish networking events I attended resulted in more business for my Search Business.*

Fast forward to today...

I no longer attend tiresome networking events, yet I have more relationships with my target market than I have ever had before because of LinkedIn.

THIS is why Recruitment/Search Business owners who master the art of relationship building on LinkedIn prosper and those who don't... DON'T!

Conclusion

How many books have you got on marketing and generating business for Recruitment/Search Businesses within 20 feet of your desk?

One? Five? Ten? Fifty?

But how many have you *actually read*?

And how many have you put to use in your Recruitment/Search business?

How many money-making ideas have you tried and tested?

This is an important point... are you using the ideas that are right there at your fingertips?

Hopefully you are.

Hopefully, you're one of the 20% of Recruitment/Search business owners that devours knowledge and tests new ideas every day.

If that's YOU, then awesome! And you're a leader in your field.

But for most Recruitment/Search business owners, they're just too busy. So their books will sit there, gathering dust on the shelves until the day when they're finally shipped off to a charity shop.

It's quite sad really, because while the books are lying idle, those Recruitment/Search business owners are having sleepless nights worrying about how the bills are going to be paid, and are frustrated that their businesses are not giving them the lifestyle they so desire.

So - if your shelves are filled with unread books, I've got some *good* and *bad* news:

The good news is, you're not alone - your competitors do it too. They'll have a mad half hour on Amazon or in a local book shop, stocking up with the best of intentions...then they'll push it all to one side while life and business gets in the way.

But the bad news is, it's costing you dearly, in terms of lost opportunities and lost revenue, and having a negative impact on your relationships with those dear to you. Because you're part of the epidemic known as *'Personal Shelf Development'*.

I've seen and heard so many Recruitment/Search business owners put growing their businesses on the back burner while they do what they always do and say things like, *"All this marketing stuff makes sense, but I am too busy at the moment"*.

WTF?

Look, there is never a perfect day to start learning and implementing new stuff that is going to grow your business.

The only perfect day is the one you're living in now.

So, answer these questions;

1. What's the most important thing you need to achieve in your business?

2. What do you need to do that you are not doing, to take your business where you want it to go?

3. When would be a good time to start doing what needs to be done?

If that big unsolved problem in your business is lead generation, then go to www.drewcoaching.com/LinkedIn-book.

References

Drew Edwards, author- Magnetic Marketing for Coaches Trainers and Consultants.

Dan Kennedy, author-The Phenomenon Achieve More in the Next 12 Months.

Claude C. Hopkins, author - My Life in Advertising & Scientific Advertising.

Jon McCulloch, author- Grow Your Business Fast.

Richard Koch, author-The 80-20 Principle.

Acknowledgements

Did you know that if you jumped off the bridge in Paris, you'd be in Seine?

And I must confess, I did question my own sanity when I decided to write my third book for the Recruitment and Search industry.

After the pain and (at times) tortuous agony of my first book 'The 7 Deadly Threats To Your Recruitment or Search Firm' I said never again would I put myself through that. Yet, less than 12 months later, I had completed my second book, 'The Persuasion, Influencing & Sales Recipe for Recruitment & Search Firm Owners' and now here I am with my third.

You will be well aware there is a tendency amongst authors to acknowledge every single person who may have influenced them in putting their book together. I'm never really convinced that you want to know that, so I am going to acknowledge those that have really helped me create this book.

I have got to start with my wife Sandra, who lets me lock myself away in the study for hours on end and puts up with my cursing and frustration. Of course my two youngest boys, who quite frankly couldn't care less about the writing and just want to share with me what is important to them. Thanks boys. And my oldest son and business partner Drew, who did most of the hard work for me.

Thanks to Samantha Gallagher for using her excellent command of abusive language to question my writing skills and to ensure that I can be the best I can be.

As I mentioned earlier, I do wonder sometimes if it is worth all the time and effort putting these books together. The thing that keeps me going, is the wonderful feedback and rave reviews I get from those in the Recruitment/Search industry from across the world. Thank you so much.

Last and not least, I wish to thank and acknowledge an old friend Alan Spooner, who when I told him I was going to write another book said, "Terry, whatever you do avoid clichés like the plague, they're so old hat!"

CPSIA information can be obtained
at www.ICGtesting.com
Printed in the USA
BVHW051459010720
582758BV00009B/383